THE COMPLETE IDIOT'S GUIDE® TO

Green Cleaning

Second Edition

*by Mary Findley
and Linda Formichelli*

ALPHA

A member of Penguin Group (USA) Inc.

This book is dedicated to all my customers, especially those in my early cleaning years, who allowed me to care for their homes. The knowledge I share with you in this book stems from those earliest roots.

 Printed on recycled paper

ALPHA BOOKS

Published by the Penguin Group

Penguin Group (USA) Inc., 375 Hudson Street, New York, New York 10014, USA

Penguin Group (Canada), 90 Eglinton Avenue East, Suite 700, Toronto, Ontario M4P 2Y3, Canada (a division of Pearson Penguin Canada Inc.)

Penguin Books Ltd., 80 Strand, London WC2R 0RL, England

Penguin Ireland, 25 St. Stephen's Green, Dublin 2, Ireland (a division of Penguin Books Ltd.)

Penguin Group (Australia), 250 Camberwell Road, Camberwell, Victoria 3124, Australia (a division of Pearson Australia Group Pty. Ltd.)

Penguin Books India Pvt. Ltd., 11 Community Centre, Panchsheel Park, New Delhi—110 017, India

Penguin Group (NZ), 67 Apollo Drive, Rosedale, North Shore, Auckland 1311, New Zealand (a division of Pearson New Zealand Ltd.)

Penguin Books (South Africa) (Pty.) Ltd., 24 Sturdee Avenue, Rosebank, Johannesburg 2196, South Africa

Penguin Books Ltd., Registered Offices: 80 Strand, London WC2R 0RL, England

International Standard Book Number: 978-1-59257-856-6
Library of Congress Catalog Card Number: 2008935069

11 10 09   8 7 6 5 4 3 2 1

Interpretation of the printing code: The rightmost number of the first series of numbers is the year of the book's printing; the rightmost number of the second series of numbers is the number of the book's printing. For example, a printing code of 09-1 shows that the first printing occurred in 2009.

Printed in the United States of America

Note: This publication contains the opinions and ideas of its authors. It is intended to provide helpful and informative material on the subject matter covered. It is sold with the understanding that the authors and publisher are not engaged in rendering professional services in the book. If the reader requires personal assistance or advice, a competent professional should be consulted.

The authors and publisher specifically disclaim any responsibility for any liability, loss, or risk, personal or otherwise, which is incurred as a consequence, directly or indirectly, of the use and application of any of the contents of this book.

Most Alpha books are available at special quantity discounts for bulk purchases for sales promotions, premiums, fund-raising, or educational use. Special books, or book excerpts, can also be created to fit specific needs.

For details, write: Special Markets, Alpha Books, 375 Hudson Street, New York, NY 10014.

Publisher: *Marie Butler-Knight*
Editorial Director: *Mike Sanders*
Senior Managing Editor: *Billy Fields*
Acquisitions Editor: *Michele Wells*
Development Editor: *Julie Bess*

Senior Production Editor: *Janette Lynn*
Copy Editor: *Megan Wade*
Cartoonist: *Chris Sabatino*
Cover Designer: *Bill Thomas*

Book Designer: *Trina Wurst*
Indexer: *Brad Herriman*
Layout: *Chad Dressler*
Proofreader: *Laura Caddell*

Contents at a Glance

Contents

Introduction

A list of "Life Is" statements was released in 1998 by "The Motivator." The first one reads: "Life Is a Challenge. Meet It." Then they challenge you a bit further: "Life Is an Adventure. Dare It," and another favorite states, "Life Is an Opportunity. Take It."

The focus of this book is to teach you how to rid your life of toxic cleaners and "green" up your cleaning act. As "The Motivator" puts it so well, you will be challenged to make vital changes. You will start on an adventure of your lifetime that will land you on a healthy, healing path. You will be encouraged to take every opportunity to move out of your comfort zone and greet a new way of walking on our Mother Earth.

You will find yourself relishing a sparkling clean home after learning Mary's cleaning tricks and shortcuts. Did we forget to mention the money savings you'll reap with Mary's formulas for homemade, Earth-friendly cleaners?

How This Book Is Organized

This book is organized in four parts.

In **Part 1, "Ready, Set, Go Green!,"** you will find the basics to green cleaning your home and the equipment you need to get it done in a jiffy. You will be taken through the steps to rid your home of toxic cleaners and clear the clutter. You'll learn the health issues caused by various cleaners, how some "organic" cleaners aren't really organic, and ways to spot the difference. There is even a chapter that teaches you how to make your own cleaners. Finally, you'll get the rundown on what to clean and how often it needs cleaning.

In **Part 2, "Room-by-Room Cleaning Guide,"** you'll receive a room-by-room guided tour of your house, including Mary's time-tested and proven cleaning methods. You'll know which product to use in each room of your home, including the kitchen, bathroom, living room, and bedroom.

In **Part 3, "The Big Stuff,"** you'll learn how to turn those big cleaning challenges into *faits accomplis*—that's French for "a walk in the park."

The French also suggest that after you finish these projects—the windows, walls, deck, floors, and more—you treat yourself to a night out.

Finally, in **Part 4, "That's Not All, Folks: Other Cleaning Challenges,"** you'll conquer everything from those laundry day blues to cleaning Fluffy and Fido to hitting a hole-in-one with a clean golf club to caring for the kids' things like stuffed animals and high chairs.

Then sit back and breathe a little easier after you rid your home of air polluters like air fresheners and dirty ducts. You'll find yourself snooping around the garden center when you learn about the plants that keep your home fresh—naturally. Oh, but don't stop until you learn Mary's new Precision Speed Cleaning methods. She'll have you zipping through house cleaning in record time.

Some Things to Help You Along the Way

To add to the material in the main text of the book, we've included sidebars that contain items you can use to understand and implement the information in this book.

Mary's Handy Hints

These tips represent Mary's 12 years of cleaning experience. They'll help you make quick work of housework.

def•i•ni•tion

These explain definitions of terms used in the text that you might not be familiar with.

Cleaning Quips

Find out what famous writers, actors, and comedians have to say about the art of housework. Some of these will give you a good chuckle as you're cleaning the toilet!

Dirty Words

Warning! Warning! This box contains cautions about cleaning pitfalls that can cause you to lose time, lose money, or—worse—lose some of the precious items in your home.

Acknowledgments

Mary's acknowledgments: Nothing is ever achieved without the dedication and assistance of many people.

Linda Formichelli; without Linda asking me to assist her on the first book, I would not have had the opportunity to rewrite the book to Green Cleaning. I missed your humor, talent, and guidance on this revision Linda. Thank you for the opportunity and for being such a great teacher! You are one of a kind.

My gratitude to Michele Wells, acquisitions editor, and Julie Bess, development editor, for your guidance and vision during the writing of this book—it would not be if it were not for you; Janette Lynn, senior production editor, for your valuable insights; and to Marilyn Allen, my agent—thank you for offering me this golden opportunity.

To my husband, Reid Findley, who took over and handled the house while my fingers happily played on these keyboards. To Paul and Ann Ensch, my parents, whose unrelenting faith in me has guided me to meet and exceed each new challenge. To my grandchildren, Gracie and Joshua, this book is for your "greener" tomorrows—you are the world to me.

To all of you who have sat through my seminars and have shared your tips; supported my company; and brought your laughter, hugs, and warmth into my life. You are a true blessing, and I am eternally grateful.

Linda's acknowledgments: I would like to thank the following people who helped make this book—and my writing dreams—come true: co-author Mary Findley; editor Michele Wells; development editor Julie Bess; my agent, Marilyn Allen; my husband, W. Eric Martin; my goal buddy, Jennifer Lawler; my parents, Anthony and Janet Formichelli; and my parents-in-law, Judith and Walter Martin.

Special Thanks to the Technical Reviewer

A special thank you to Theresa Peterson owner of "Maid to Order" Cleaning Services and director of the Independent Cleaners Purchasing

Alliance who checked the accuracy of the information contained in *The Complete Idiot's Guide® to Green Cleaning.* You can read this book with the confidence that what you learn about green cleaning is correct and precise.

Trademarks

All terms mentioned in this book that are known to be or are suspected of being trademarks or service marks have been appropriately capitalized. Alpha Books and Penguin Group (USA) Inc. cannot attest to the accuracy of this information. Use of a term in this book should not be regarded as affecting the validity of any trademark or service mark.

Ready, Set, Go Green!

In the late 1960s, a movement began among college students referred to as "The Age of Aquarius." It was a time of rebellion against the war in Vietnam, the ideological ways of our culture, and treatment of women.

People today are also rebelling, but against the use of toxic cleaners, flame and stain retardants in furniture, and chemicals being added to water supplies and food. It's called "The Green Movement." In this section you will learn how all aspects of the green movement pull together to form a powerful and healthy ally. Embrace the entirety of the Movement and "Let the Sunshine In."

Prep School: Going Green to Clean

In This Chapter

- ◆ Toxic buildup is all about time
- ◆ Listen, learn, apply
- ◆ Reaping the green rewards
- ◆ Toss it once and for all

In days of long ago, our Native Peoples never thought about restoring Mother Earth either locally or on a global level. To them it was unconscionable to destroy the earth. They took only what they needed for survival, leaving no trace behind them.

Yet within 100 very short years, our thirst for material goods has nearly extinguished the bounties of Mother Earth. Some people feel the damage is beyond being reversible.

Kermit the Frog once sang "It's not easy being green." Well Kermit, hopefully we all can learn to be as green as you.

Throughout this chapter, you will read the makings of a good mystery thriller. The twisted lies, strange words, and diversion tactics some companies pull add up to a who-done-it—you'll learn where the crime was committed and with what weapon.

A good counterattack starts with basic training at MAS—Mary's Awareness School—where you'll learn to sharpen your sleuthing skills.

Join the Green Revolution

All this talk of going green sounds like a year-round St. Patrick's Day parade. By opening this book, you decided to join the celebration. By implementing a few of these suggestions, you and Mother Earth will reap tenfold that of your efforts.

The small stuff might not count elsewhere, but when your health and that of Mother Earth is involved, the small stuff counts. As you walk down the green road, be prepared to notice little things like improved health, being able to smell the roses (your sinuses should clear up), increased energy, and no more clutter.

Small Changes = Huge Benefits

The White Rabbit in *Alice in Wonderland* stomped and bellowed "It's late, it's late, it's really, really late," then disappeared down a hole. Exactly how late it is to reverse the damage done to Mother Earth no one knows.

Please spare the whining about how one person can't make a difference. The author of this book is only one person yet with the mops she has sold over the years, she has kept more than 500,000 mops out of the landfills—and saved the energy and natural resources that would have been used to manufacture them.

Put Old Habits to Rest

From spiritual leaders to politicians to songwriters, we have been encouraged throughout the years to climb out of that hole and make changes in our lives. Bob Dylan, Martin Luther King, and President

John Kennedy all encouraged strength and courage to make personal changes for the good of all mankind.

The vital changes you are about to make put you at better odds of never hearing those dreadful words "You have cancer." Think of cancer like a diet. To lose weight you must stop eating the food that causes you to gain weight. To help prevent cancer you must stop using the products that cause it.

 Dirty Words

The American Cancer Society estimated that nearly 1,445,000 new cases of cancer cropped up last year. They also estimate that nearly 40 percent of all Americans will contract some kind of cancer.

Green means Go. It doesn't mean sitting through the stoplight with old habits hanging around your neck while everyone behind you honks their irritations. It means stepping on the gas to make changes.

Is Going Green going to hurt? No. Will you enjoy newfound health? Yes. Is Going Green going to cost? Yes, in terms of a little bit of effort and replacing toxic chemicals, personal care products, and food with healthy alternatives. The overall monetary investment is minuscule compared to the alternative cost of cancer and ill health.

A New Way of Thinking

Growing up in Missouri, people often told me, "You are as stubborn as a Missouri mule." Stubbornness can indicate a resistant nature. People tend to hold onto comfortable old ways, which are familiar.

The old ways are not working. That is why 40 percent of our population faces cancer. If what you are doing isn't working, then change you must. Family members might resist when you begin to go green. Toss them the sales pitch of your life. If you need to learn how, listen to your kids. They pitch you every second of every day, and they are darn good at it.

The four most valuable words in our language are "I need your help." Use them often when asking your family to do their part in greening your home.

Going green is an exciting new way of thinking, acting, and being in our world. It is a breath of fresh air in a stagnant world. Prince Phillip of England once said, "Change does not change tradition. It strengthens it. Change is a challenge and an opportunity, not a threat."

You Reap What You Use

During my professional cleaning years, a seal of approval was an alien life form and ammonia was the staple cleaner. No one questioned whether the fumes could destroy your lungs, your mental capacities, and usually both.

Today unless a product carries the Green Seal of Approval, the toxins in that cleaner can be far more dangerous than the ammonia or lye used back then.

When it comes to chemicals, what you don't know will hurt you. One whiff of an open bottle of ammonia and your nose tells you that it is not a safe cleaner to be using. Chemical manufacturers caught onto these sniffing techniques and now camouflage the toxic odors of their "brews" with scents such as "spring fresh" or "autumn rain." Your nose no longer knows the difference between safe or possible carcinogenic compounds.

Dirty Words

Look at the back of your hair shampoo, hand lotion, or other personal care item bottles for the words *sodium hydroxide* or *sodium laurel sulfate*. Nearly every personal care product contains one of them, yet both are toxic chemicals.

Will one toxic chemical cause illness or cancer? Probably not. More often it is a matter of buildup. Let's say your carpet is stained. First, you use Zout stain remover. The stain remains, so you try Go Getem. Nothing. Frustrated, you pour on Spot BeGone.

The air-conditioning was running, so you kept the windows closed. All three cleaners soaked into your hands. You inhaled the fumes, contaminating your lungs. Your face was close to the carpet, so you breathed fumes that gas off from carpeting.

Pretty ugly crime scene isn't it? The fun has just begun. Layer upon layer of toxic chemicals build in your home. Everyday someone sprays hair spray, air freshener, nonstick spray, or a cleaner in the home. Each time that spray bottle comes out so does the welcome mat for cancer, heart disease, nervous disorders, asthma, emphysema, and a host of other maladies.

The good news? There are healthy, effective alternatives.

Spray It, Breathe It

You read correctly. Sprays—especially aerosols—linger in the air for several days. That means daily shower cleaners, hair spray, and air fresheners used day after day never go away. Sprays also go into your lungs more easily as you inhale the little droplets.

Everyone has problems getting hairspray off a bathroom countertop. Ponder this for just a second. If you can't get the sticky hairspray off your bathroom counters, how do you expect to get it off your lungs and liver and out of your arteries?

When fumes become overpowering in a home, you throw open the windows to air out the house, such as when you paint. You can't just throw open your body and air it out. Your body has no way to rid itself of these toxins.

According to the American Lung Association, common symptoms of using sprays in the home include:

- Headaches, fatigue, shortness of breath, and dizziness
- Worsening allergy and asthma symptoms
- Sinus congestion, cough, and sneezing
- Eye, nose, throat, and skin irritation

> **Cleaning Quips**
>
> The Environmental Protection Agency (EPA) reports, "Long-term exposure to some indoor air pollutants can lead to damage of the central nervous system, kidneys, and liver."

Wipe On, Wipe Off

After reading the last section, you must be asking yourself if it means I'm putting the ax to using sprays. Um, yes I am.

In the first *Karate Kid* movie, Pat Morita taught Ralph Macchio to wax a car by "wax on—wax off." "Wax on—wax off" works quite well when cleaning your home, too. Stop the habit of spraying a cleaner directly on a surface, especially vertical surfaces. When you spray a vertical surface, the spray drifts right into your face. Even on a flat surface, a spray drifts into the air.

Mary's Handy Hints

Not sure whether your personal care products are toxic? Check your products at www. safecosmetics.org. Click "How safe are your beauty products?" and then click the tab labeled "skin deep."

Pour the cleaner onto a cloth and then wipe down the surface. Wait a minute and wipe with a dry cloth. Should you need to spray a cloth, spray downward into the cloth. It is safer to spray a cloth than a surface because the cloth catches the droplets.

Let's explore alternatives for some of the more popular sprays used in your home.

◆ Stuck on hairspray? Switch to a gel like Aubrey that is chemical free. Many of the toxic chemicals used in cleaners are also found in body care products. So go au-natural.

◆ Replace nonstick food sprays with liquid olive oil.

◆ Pull the plug on plug-in air fresheners and air freshener sprays. Open the windows, try Pure Ayre (an enzyme air freshener), or place spices around the room in bowls.

◆ Substitute aerosol deodorants with solids.

◆ Starch shirts with a mixture of 1 teaspoon of cornstarch per half cup of water. Mix thoroughly in a spritz bottle, which puts out far fewer droplets than a sprayer.

Ransack Your Home

Here comes that "dirty" word *change* again. People accuse me of being worse than a mother eagle when it comes to changing their bad habits. Mother eagles use their wings to continuously knock their young out of the nest until they learn to fly. Sometimes we, too, need to be knocked out of our comfortable nest when learning new ways.

Grab several heavy plastic bags, strong boxes, and your digital camera. Head into areas such as your garage, attic, closets, shed, or anywhere "stuff" is stored.

Old things collect mold, dust, dust mites, pollen, mice, cockroaches, ants, raccoons, bats, and who knows what else that has sought out your garage, attic, and shed for a nice undisturbed piece of real estate. If you suspect rodents or mold, wear gloves and protective clothing. Remove all clothing before you go inside your home; otherwise, you will spread the contamination to the inside of your home.

Mary's Handy Hints

When was the last time you took pictures of all your possessions in case of fire or flooding? You are about to clear the clutter out of your home. Take advantage of this time as you sort boxes to do a bit of multitasking and get your pictures up-to-date.

You might want to clean as you clear the areas, so take along your cleaners and wet or dry vacuum. As you clear the clutter, keep in mind the time test. Have you used the item in the past 12–18 months? Does it have family value? Do you really need it?

If you don't need the item, give it to Goodwill or have a garage sale. There are talented people who can create art from our clutter. I'm not one of them, though, so don't ask me to take your leftovers!

As you start clearing out clutter and toxic chemicals, tackle the most important areas first like the garage. My stamina and tolerance is revved up at the beginning of a project. By the time I'm midway through, though, I could care less if a 20-year-old pair of pants ever comes down out of that attic.

Garage, Attic, and Shed

With some products, the 12-month test can be nixed. Paint is a prime example. Dispose of paints only if they smell, have rusted, appear to have mold on top of them, or are hard.

Mary's Handy Hints

Make sure your paint cans are properly sealed by turning them upside down in a plastic bucket. Reseal the lid if any paint drips out so the paint stays fresh.

Check paint thinners, turpentine, or things like wood putty for signs of rust and the "use by" date listed on the container. If they don't smell and aren't hard, they have life left in them.

Next, grab all the cleaners within reach. Most powdered and liquid cleaners will last several years, except in high humidity. If the product's odor has changed or a film or obvious mildew is floating on top, take it to the Hazardous Waste Collection Site along with any powder that has hardened.

Get rid of any clear plastic that has yellowed. This plastic has oxidized and is giving off toxic fumes. Take old plastic containers and out-of-date electronic gadgets to the recycler.

Properly dispose of anything that has molded. Wrap the object in a plastic bag to prevent the mold from spreading.

Closets and Cabinets

Pick out your worst cluttered cabinet and closet. Apply my three Cs: clear, clean, and consolidate. Each week as you clean the kitchen, tackle one cabinet. A month later you'll have space to hide some of the countertop clutter.

As you clear your cabinets, look at expiration dates and rusted or bulging cans. Replace anything plastic with glass, ceramic, or stainless steel. Plastic leaches toxins into your food, which worsens each time it is run through the dishwasher.

Open up your flour, sugar, oats, cereals, and anything that moths, bugs, or mice would nibble. Take a close look at shelves and closet floors for evidence of mice or cockroaches.

Each month dedicate half a day to a closet. Sort through boxes and remove any moldy items or those that have an odor. Immediately place moldy items in a plastic bag so you don't spread the mold throughout your home. Look for critter droppings, moths, or ant invasions. Treat these infestations with nontoxic products found at natural garden supply stores or health food stores.

Mary's Handy Hints

Rather than being a part of the pollution problem, go green and be a part of the solution. Start your own family volunteer program to reduce and reuse.

Proper Disposal

Never throw chemicals, cleaners, medicine, or any other product down your drain or into your toilet. Store them safely until you have enough for a trip to the toxic waste dump.

Researchers have found unsafe and shockingly high levels of medicines in the water samples of a dozen large cities. The old saying "you are what you eat" also applies to water. City municipal water systems cannot handle the overload of toxins dumped into the drainage system. What you pour down your drains and into your toilet comes back into your water supply unless you are on a well.

If your city does not have curbside pickup for recyclable items, get your neighbors together and take turns taking recyclables to the recycle center. Glass; plastic (except the number 6); all papers (including newspaper and magazines) should be taken to your recycling center. Oil, paint, and any toxic chemicals, fertilizer, bug spray, and so forth should be taken to the Hazardous Waste Collection Site.

Adopt the habit of marking the date of purchase of any item that might be stored for a period of time, such as cleaners, paint, spices, and so forth, on the side of the container. This tells you the age of the item and gives you a good idea of when to replace it.

Simplify Your Life

As small children, we filled our pockets with pill bugs, rocks, worms, or any interesting little critter that we could crowd into those pockets.

Gratefully, the washing machine rinsed away the smushed ones in our back pockets. The habit of "collecting things" continues throughout our life.

Clothing gets tucked away in the attic because someone might want that jacket. We walk through department stores grabbing gadgets off the end aisles that are sold for a quarter in a garage sale five years later.

Mary's Handy Hints

Just say *no* to impulse buying. Stick to what is on your list. Impulse buying is costly to you and the environment.

As long as you are greening your cleaning, jump feet first into greening your lifestyle through simplification.

Let's take a quick look at the entire manufacturing process to give you an inside view as to the wasted energy it takes to make one piece of clothing.

Everything on Earth is made from some kind of raw material—even if the item is remanufactured from recycled parts like microfiber, which is recycled plastic pop bottles that originated from oil. First, you need energy to operate the machinery and power to extract the raw material. Don't forget the energy, material, and the subsequent waste needed to manufacture the machinery.

The raw material is shipped to the manufacturing plant by a truck, which uses fuel and which costs to manufacture. At the factory, more energy and machinery are required to manufacture the item. Don't forget the raw materials and energy used to make the manufacturing equipment.

After being boxed with cardboard from a tree that was once the home and food source for many creatures (don't forget the fuel and material needed to cut down the tree), another truck hauls the product to a general warehouse. Yet another truck is needed to take it to the store. You then consume fuel driving to the store, where the item is placed in a paper bag from yet another tree for you to take it home.

The semi trucks hauling the goods average maybe 7 miles per gallon. Then there is the fuel and gas fumes from the forklifts and the building space and electricity for storage.

Follow the direction of our Native Americans. Take only what you need, leaving no footprints behind you.

The Least You Need to Know

- ◆ The buildup of toxic chemicals and gases in your home contributes to a multitude of health issues.

- ◆ There is no more important job than that of caring for ourselves, our children, and our Mother Earth.

- ◆ Discard, recycle, or sell any item you have not used in the past 12 months—exceptions noted.

- ◆ Apply the 3 Rs of Green Cleaning: reduce, resist, and research before you buy.

Chapter 2

The Hit List

In This Chapter

- ◆ Know your stuff
- ◆ The worst offenders
- ◆ Deciphering labels and MSDS sheets
- ◆ Organic does not always mean safe

The Complete Idiot's Guide books are treasured for their light-hearted approach to a variety of informative subjects. However, this chapter circumvents humor to discuss major health issues connected to toxic chemicals used in many cleaners.

You are also taken on a detour to the toxins emitted from furniture, drapes, and flooring. What I call a "sick home" is a compilation of many toxins, not just those emitted by chemicals.

You'll learn how to decipher labels and read *MSDS* sheets with the eye of a detective.

def•i•ni•tion

MSDS stands for Material Safety Data Sheet. Provided by the manufacturer, MSDS sheets disclose toxic chemicals above a certain level, their hazards, warnings, and safety precautions.

When "Green" Is Black

Have you ever had one of those days when you slapped your head because you overlooked an important detail? My poor head took another smack one day after picking up a bottle of treatment for *holding tanks* for RVs and boats.

The front of the label read *biodegradable*. Taking care of Mother Earth is foremost to me, and I always assumed that because a product is biodegradable it is safe to use. Then I saw "Caution: Poison" and flipped the bottle over to read the back. There in small letters it read "Caution contains formaldehyde."

def•i•ni•tion

RVs and boats have both "gray" and "black" **holding tanks.** Gray tanks hold water that comes from faucets and showers. Black tanks hold the stuff from toilets. Products are used in the tanks to keep them from smelling like a portable potty.

Doesn't biodegradable mean that a product is safe for the environment? No, it does not. Many chemicals biodegrade into even more dangerous chemicals, especially if they come into contact with other chemicals. Some products, like styrofoam, never biodegrade and leave what are called footprints on Mother Earth.

How biodegradable is a product? It would take a Ph.D. in chemistry to know those answers. Some chemicals biodegrade in a few days; others take hundreds of years. Never assume a product is Earth and human friendly because it's biodegradable.

A product's claim to be human and Earth friendly means about as much as a product being biodegradable. "Organic" product manufacturers are under the same guidelines as other manufacturers. They can say what they want on a bottle with little or no accountability. Look for your Green Seals of Approval and other like designations.

As you learn about going green, keep in mind that some of these toxic chemicals bioaccumulate or build up in your body. Dioxin is one of them. It is a fat-soluble chemical stored forever in your body.

Earlier you learned that one chemical used a few times might not cause health issues. It takes consistent exposure for most problems to surface. By the time they do, though, the damage is done often without symptoms.

Dirty Words

Silicone is one example of how a chemical changes. When it is mixed 50/50 with water—a normal mixture in car wax products—and then heated to a temperature of 150°F, it turns into formaldehyde and silicate dioxide. Temperatures inside a semi truck that hauls these chemicals often exceeds 150°F during summer months.

The Environmental Protection Agency (EPA) calls this buildup body burden. It is the burden our body carries as a result of repeated exposure to fat-soluble products. Because the chemical does not break down, it is called persistent and bioaccumulates inside your body. Dioxin is a good example.

According to the *Extension Toxicology Network*, "Bioaccumulation means an increase in the concentration of a chemical in a biological organism over time. Compounds accumulate in living things any time they are taken up and stored faster than they are broken down (metabolized) or excreted."

Further, that accumulation moves up the food chain, resulting in biomagnification. Simply put, say plankton absorbs dioxin from the water. Shrimp, which also absorb dioxin from the water, eat the plankton. Fish, which also absorb dioxin from water, eat the shrimp. We then eat the fish, adding to the already existing layers of dioxin we have previously absorbed.

def•i•ni•tion

The **Extension Toxicology Network** is a Pesticide Information Project of the Extension Offices of Cornell University, Oregon State University, University of Idaho, University of California at Davis, and Michigan State University.

Now that you know the basic background of a few important words that will cross your path, let's get face-to-face with the dirty side of these cleaners.

The Silent Killers

We grow up thinking of home as our safety net. People set aside a special room or quiet spot where the rest of the world vanishes. In their quiet space, the ills of the world cannot touch them, or so they think. Unless you carefully chose your furnishings from flooring to the paint on the walls, your home could be full of elements that cause cancer and a host of other maladies.

Manufacturing companies are not required to tell you the contents of their products. The warning labels on liquids are vague at best and nonexistent on clothing, carpeting, and furniture. Physical problems don't crop up for years. By the time they rear their ugly heads, it is too late.

Prevention is the key to halting cancer, nerve damage, kidney and liver problems, as well as other ailments caused by everyday products we presume are safe.

Dirty Words

Should you choose to have new carpet installed, stay away from your home during installation and two to three days afterwards to allow some of the fumes to off-gas. Ventilate well. More than 100 chemicals are used to make carpet, and they can cause neurological damage to the brain. Symptoms include headaches, nausea, depression, memory loss, and injury to the thyroid gland and immune system. Children have had epileptic seizures from playing on newly laid carpet. Better yet, choose safe flooring such as wool or real wood.

You will read the word *prevention* repeatedly throughout this book. It is the key to good health. Face it: we all picture ourselves as being as beautiful as the models in the hair shampoo commercials; that the most dazzling of white teeth can be ours by using the latest toothpaste; or that our countertops will glimmer with the latest cleaner.

Let's take a quick look at some evils lurking in your home.

♦ **Mighty Suds shampoo leaves your hair shimmering.** A closer look at the ingredients will show that it contains sodium laurel sulfate. This nasty little chemical reacts with the plastic bottle, forming toxic nitrates and dioxins that leach into your body every time you shampoo your hair.

♦ **You might want to buy the newest fashion of vinyl flooring.** Vinyl flooring is made from polyvinyl chloride (PVC), vinyl chloride monomer, and ethylene dichloride. These products release literally tons of toxic chemicals every year into the environment. Those chemicals march into your home along with the vinyl flooring. Linoleum is a far safer choice.

♦ **You can't wait to get your new vinyl recliner.** Vinyl flooring and vinyl furniture leach phthalates, which reduce sperm counts in men and damage the liver and kidneys. The off-gassing from stain retardants added to furniture fabric is discussed in Chapter 16.

Grab your microscope and follow closely as we traipse through stores for a closer look into the dangers behind cleaners, personal care products, furniture, and flooring.

First up is a look into a few misguided concepts about cleaners.

Hidden Danger

Ignorance is *not* bliss when it comes to your health. What you don't know can make you ill. Arm yourself with determination and knowledge, with the goal to rid your life of the toxins within your control.

Chemical companies are not required to state the contents of their cleaners on a bottle. This section reveals various dangerous chemicals commonly found in cleaners, soaps, and laundry detergents. Although body care product ingredients are not listed, many of these chemicals are found in bath soap, shampoo, makeup, perfume, hair spray, and deodorant. Do your research and know what is in your product before using it.

Dirty Words _____

Mary's Formula: Multiple products + buildup + time = health issues.

Also be aware of the numerous products that contain chlorine. You'll find it in laundry detergent, all-purpose cleaners, dish soaps, and in the water from your faucets if you are on a city sewer system.

Cleaners, Soaps, and Detergents

The following lists the separate groups of cleaners, the various chemicals found in them, and the health issues they cause.

Glass and Window Cleaners: 2-butoxyethanol or butyl cellosolve, alcohols, ammonia, anionic surfactant, ethanolamine, ethylene glycol butyl ether (EGBE), isobutane, naphtha, phosphoric acid, and synthetic dyes and scents.

Health problems: Naphtha and EGBE cause respiratory problems and liver and kidney damage and depress the central nervous system, causing mental confusion; suspected carcinogens; eye and severe skin irritations, asthma, and lung problems; fatal if swallowed.

All-Purpose Cleaners, Carpet Spot Removers, Carpet Cleaners: Ammonia, bleach, butyl cellusolve or 2-butoxyethanol, chlorides, diethanolamine, ethers, ethylene glycol, hydroxyacetic acid, hydroxides, limonene (d-limonene, 4-isopropenyl-1-methylcyclohexene), morpholine (extremely toxic), naphtha, perchloroethylene (tetrachloroethylene; ethylene tetrachloride etroleum); petroleum distillates, phenols, phosphoric acid, trisodium phosphate (TSP), volatile organic compounds (VOCs).

Health problems: Irritants to eyes, can cause blindness; fatal if swallowed; headaches, nausea, neurological damage, memory loss; suspected carcinogens; neurotoxins; damage to blood, kidneys, and liver; severe burning of the skin; overexposure to phosphoric acid is deadly; petroleum distillates are flammable and carcinogenic.

In addition, if an all-purpose cleaner, soap, or detergent is antibacterial, it probably contains triclosan. Absorption through the skin has been tied to liver damage.

Dirty Words

For the sake of the environment and your health, stop using anti-bacterial products. They do not kill germs. Wash your hands with soap and water upon returning home, after using the restroom, and before handling food to protect you against germs.

Antibacterial cleaners and soaps washed into your sewer system or septic system kill the enzymes that eat bacteria and solid waste matter. Why kill the most valuable defense against germs?

Bathroom Cleaners: Ammonia and ammonia chlorides, chlorine bleach, diethylene glycol monobutyl ether, glycosides, hydroxides, limonene (d-limonene, 4-isopropenyl-1-methylcyclohexene), naphtha, petroleum distillates, phenols, phosphoric acid, trisodium phosphate (TSP).

Health problems: See all-purpose cleaners.

Toilet Bowl Cleaner: Hydrochloric acid, hypochlorite, bleach, ammonia, diethanolamine, napthalene.

Health problems: Highly corrosive, irritant to skin, eyes, and respiratory tract; damages liver and kidneys; may cause vomiting or coma if ingested. Causes chlorine fumes when combined with other chemicals, which is fatal. Napthalene can cause cataracts, corneal damage, and kidney damage; is extremely toxic to small children and infants; and is a suspected carcinogen.

Laundry Detergent: Alkylate sulfonate, calcium (sodium) hypocrite, sodium tripolyphosphate and potassium metabisulfite, ethylene-diamine-tetra-acetic (EDTA) and diammonium.

Health problems: Highly corrosive, irritates or burns skin and mucous membranes, eyes, and respiratory tract; liver damage; vomiting; is absorbed by the skin from clothing, causing allergies, asthma, and skin rashes; does not readily biodegrade.

Many powdered laundry detergents contain saw dust, which is used as a filler. It does not dissolve and it clogs drains, causes skin irritations, and cannot clean your clothes.

Dish Soap and Dishwasher Detergent: Chlorine, limonene or d-limonene, diethanolamine (DEA), sodium hypochlorite (sodium hydroxide or lye).

Health problems: Skin irritations; phosphates pollute the groundwater; carcinogenic.

Floor Cleaners: 2-butoxyethanol, ammonium hydroxide, dipropylene glycol methyl ether, monoethanolamine, nonylphenol polyethoxylate.

Health problems: Eye, skin, and lung irritants; damage the respiratory tract, endocrine system, and central nervous system.

Dirty Words

Read labels! Look for words such as *sodium dioxide.* It is found in medicine, food, carpeting, clothing, drink bottles, herbicides, cleaners, and even hand lotions. This dangerous chemical causes cancer, mental illness, and diabetes, for starters. Burning or heating plastic releases the chemical into the air. Never heat food in the microwave in plastic or freeze water in plastic bottles.

The Rest of What Ails You

Phew, you just read an eye full of information. Take a deep breath because we are about to expose other toxins that weasel their way into your cabinets.

Furniture Polish, Floor Polish: Benzene, nitrobenzene, petroleum distillates, perchloroethylene (tetrachloroethylene; ethylene tetrachloride); morpholine (extremely toxic), phenol (carbolic acid); linseed oil.

Health problems: Chronic inhalation can cause liver damage, disruption of the central nervous system, depression, and respiratory tract irritation; skin and eye irritants; never use petroleum distillates inside your home because they're flammable, as is linseed oil.

Linseed oil can contain arsenic, beryllium, chromium, cadmium, and nickel, which are known to cause cancer; the lead in linseed oil causes birth defects and other reproductive problems; upon evaporation, this oil can spontaneously combust and cause a fire; after using linseed oil, dry the cloths outside the home in the shade and then take them to the toxic waste dump; never machine wash or dry these cloths because they can catch fire.

Drain Openers: Lye, hydrochloric acid, trichloroethane.

Health problems: Caustic; burn skin and eyes; damage to esophagus if swallowed; damage kidneys, liver, and digestive tract; nervous system depressant.

Mold and Mildew Removers: Sodium hypochlorite, formaldehyde.

Health problems: Burn skin, eyes, nose, and throat; cause nausea, headaches, nose bleeds, dizziness, shortness of breath, and fluid in the lungs (which can lead to coma or death).

Oven Cleaner: Benzene, sodium hydroxide (lye).

Health problems: Caustic; strong irritant; burns to both skin and eyes; inhibits reflexes; severe tissue damage if swallowed.

Hidden and Not-So-Hidden Hazards

You pride yourself in the cleanliness of your home. You mop your floors often and vacuum the carpet regularly. What a contented feeling knowing that your children and pets have a safe place to romp and play. Or do they?

According to the Environmental Working Group, pets licking their paws ingest larger amounts of chemicals contained in vinyl and carpeted surfaces than originally believed. They have found that thyroid disease and cancer are increasing disproportionate to the general pet population.

Being young and smaller, children are more vulnerable to ill health caused by toxins than adults. They play on the floor, inhaling the off-gassing from vinyl flooring and carpeting. This disrupts the development of their organs and body systems and causes dizziness and nausea.

 Dirty Words

Pregnant women are advised never to have carpet or vinyl installed before or during the time they are pregnant or nursing. Wait until a child is much older. Stone and wood floors are safer options, but the adhesive used to lay them emits VOCs. Before you install new carpet check with www. carpet-rug.org for certified green carpets.

To complicate matters further, some cleaners react with the composition of vinyl or carpeted flooring. Clean a vinyl floor with a heavy-duty cleaner and the result is a dull floor. The cleaner has removed the shiny finish and by reacting with the chemicals in the vinyl emitted VOCs into the air. No tests have been done to determine which chemicals react with the composite material. Only your health knows for sure.

Here is an inside view into the composition of vinyl and carpeted flooring. Chapter 12 on flooring teaches the proper way to clean all floor surfaces.

The Ugly Side of Carpet, Vinyl, and Furniture

Vinyl: Polyvinyl chloride (PVC) is one of many well-known and carcinogenic additives in vinyl flooring. PVC releases chemical softeners called phthalates, which are common plastic additives. PVC flooring has been associated with increases in respiratory problems and cancer. It is highly flammable.

Another common additive to vinyl flooring is DEHP, a plasticizer used to soften plastics. DEHP can damage a developing male reproductive system and the respiratory systems of children. DEHP also causes cancer in laboratory animals.

Carpet: Carpeting contains as many as 100+ chemicals. Several off-gas within a few days of being installed, while others take years. Some of these chemicals include artificial dyes, antimicrobial treatments, antistatic sprays, petroleum by-products and synthetics (polypropylene, nylon, acrylic), PVC, soil and stain repellents, urethane, vinyl, and latex.

They can cause headaches, dizziness, or nausea.

Other chemicals in carpeting can cause far worse problems:

- **p-Dichlorobenzene.** A known carcinogenic that causes hallucinations, nerve damage, and respiratory illness.

- **4-PC (4-phenylcyclohexene or latex).** Applied to the back of carpet, it gives carpets their "new carpet smell" and is associated with eye, nose, and upper respiratory problems.

+ **Mothproofing chemicals (naphthalene).** This was discussed earlier.

+ **Fire retardants with polybrominated diphenyl ether (PBDEs).** Can cause damage to the thyroid, immune system, and brain development functions.

Most synthetic carpeting contains formaldehyde. Even the foam padding, carpet underlay, or foam in upholstery emits VOCs.

Mary's Handy Hints

The report "Sick of Dust: Chemicals in Common Products—A Needless Health Threat in Our Homes" can be found online at www.safer-products.org. The *San Francisco Tribune's* special report on pollutants in our bodies is available at www.insidebayarea.com/bodyburden.

Lurking in Your Furniture

In October 2007, Friends of the Earth, an environmental group, tested 350 pieces of household furniture in homes and stores throughout California. Not surprisingly, they found high levels of toxic halogenated fire retardants.

Babies and young children are especially vulnerable to fire retardants. These substances have been banned in children's clothing but not in furniture. Pregnant women absorb them through their skin where the toxins go directly into the unborn child.

Fire retardants bioaccumulate so what the baby receives through the placenta multiplies each time the child lies on the couch.

The worst of the offenders, brominated flame retardants (BFRs), particularly polybrominated diphenyl ether (PBDE) are found in both furniture foam and fabrics. These cancer-causing, hormone-disruptive chemicals have been found in animals and have worked their way into dairy products, poultry, and fish.

Mary's Handy Hints

Covering furniture with blankets or bath towels prevents the absorption of flame retardants through the skin.

Perfluorochemicals (PFCs) have tested positive in furniture, Teflon, Stainmaster, and Scotchguard. Perfluoroocatanic acid, a member of the perfluorochemical group, is a proven carcinogen.

Furniture sometimes is dyed with benzidine or hydrazine —also known carcinogens. Vinyl furniture contains the same toxic chemicals as vinyl flooring. Opt for real leather or switch to an alternative safe fabric furniture.

Avoid any wood furniture containing chromium copper arsenic (CCA) or creosote and wood treated with pentachlorophenol.

Only use a mild soap to remove stains from fabric furniture. The combination of the cleaner and flame retardant chemicals can cause headaches and nausea.

Understanding What You Read

No job is more difficult than finding safe cleaners for your home. Loopholes protect chemical companies from disclosing the chemical contents of their products. They get by with issuing various warnings or don't list chemicals at all.

They also disguise the names. Car waxes use names like aliphatic hydrocarbon or mineral oil for petroleum distillates. Or they tell you the content is "proprietary information."

To throw salt on an open wound, chemical companies often put two chemicals in one bottle that cause like problems. Say one chemical can mildly irritate your sinuses while another is known for causing severe asthma attacks. The company can lump the two together with a simple warning "may cause nasal irritations."

Furthermore, even if a chemical company is required to test its products, it is not required to obtain outside testing. The company can interpret its own test results conducted by its own company and determine what, if any, labels or warnings go on the bottle.

It has been well proven that indoor air pollution in your home exceeds that of any air you breathe outside. Stay-at-home women and especially mothers are far more likely to succumb to major illnesses such as cancer, hormone imbalances, memory loss, and immune deficiencies than women who work outside the home.

Mary's Handy Hints _____

Never buy any cleaner or product unless the product contents are clearly marked on the label. If you can't pronounce the words on a bottle, leave it on the shelf of the store.

This Thing Called a Label

The Federal Hazardous Substance Act (FHSA) stipulates four "trigger or signal" words to indicate hazardous content within a bottle or product. Products must carry the following warnings if applicable:

- ◆ **Caution**—Means the product is relatively nontoxic to slightly toxic.

- ◆ **Warning**—Means the product is moderately toxic.

- ◆ **Danger**—Indicates highly toxic chemicals.

- ◆ **Poison**—Tells you to ventilate the room, wear protective clothing including masks, and use every precaution necessary.

Other words you might find on a bottle include:

- ◆ **Active Ingredient**—The chemical that is responsible for doing the job you need to be handled.

- ◆ **Precautionary Statements**—List possible hazards to pets and people.

- ◆ **Environmental Hazards**—Tells you of any dangers to the environment or wildlife.

- ◆ **First Aid Statements**—These instruct you on how to handle a reaction. Call Poison Control (1-800-222-1222) for first aid.

There is yet another classification of chemicals and materials you must know. These materials and substances can contaminate, harm, or kill living organisms:

- ◆ **Toxic**—Means this product is poisonous and can be harmful to human or animal health.

- ◆ **Corrosive**—This product can corrode storage containers or damage tissue if contact is made with the product.

> ◆ **Reactive**—This product can react or explode if exposed to heat, shock, air, or water.

> ◆ **Ignitable**—Take all precautions because this substance can catch on fire, emit toxic gas or fumes, or explode.

Always read and follow the bottle's directions exactly. Never throw a substance down the drain. Take it to the toxic dump for proper disposal.

Mysterious MSDS

Material Safety Data Sheets (MSDS) are as ambiguous as bottle information. Only hazardous ingredients in amounts above 1 percent of the product are listed on MSDS sheets. Unfortunately, hundreds of chemicals in far lower concentrations can cause toxic reactions.

MSDS sheets do tell you in detail the first aid treatment for inhalation, skin irritations, and spills and provide instructions for firefighters in case of a fire. The rest of the content is so technical you might not be able to decipher the information.

Sometimes you will find a rating numbered from 0 to 4. 0 is safe, 1 is slight, 2 is moderate, 3 is high, and 4 is extreme danger. The ratings are listed for health, flammability, and reactivity or skin contact.

MSDS sheets must list a toxic chemical's Chemical Abstracts Service Registry (CAS) number. On a search engine, type "MSDS for CAS 62-9843-12" (fake number) into the search line. That brings up the MSDS sheet for that chemical for further information.

One Step at a Time

You may feel a bit overwhelmed after reading the above warnings. Remember "Going Green" is a step-by-step process. Start small by taking the steps that best suit your situation and needs.

In later chapters we'll suggest a variety of free to inexpensive ways to improve the health of your home especially with plants. When it does come time to upgrade your furniture or flooring, turn to Appendix B for healthy alternatives.

The Least You Need to Know

- Make purchasing decisions based on knowledge not advertising gimmicks.

- The words *biodegradable*, *organic*, and *Earth friendly* on a package does not guarantee it is toxin free.

- Being educated about cleaners can save your life.

- Look behind the scenes of a bottle before using its contents.

Chapter 3

Tooling Around

In This Chapter

- ◆ Choose your tools wisely
- ◆ Happy vacuuming
- ◆ The greener side of cleaners
- ◆ Rags, cloths, scrubbers, and sponges
- ◆ Sweeping you off your feet: brooms and mops

Picking out cleaning tools reminds me a bit of how I evened the score with one of my cousins down on the farm after he clobbered me with a hedge ball. Hedge balls are the size of a softball and are hard, so they leave a nasty bruise.

To retaliate, I waited until this cousin entered the outhouse. After letting him "settle in" for a minute, I pushed a firecracker under the back wall and struck a match. The resulting boom brought the cousin running out with his pants down around his knees.

Most cleaning equipment resembles ornery cousins with hedge balls. They leave nasty bruises on the surfaces they clean. Armed with the information in this chapter, though, you can keep ahead of those nasty little surprises. You'll find yourself chuckling as you pocket the cost savings and log less time on the cleaning clock.

Good Ain't Cheap and Cheap Ain't Good

"Good ain't cheap and cheap ain't good." What does this sales slogan have to do with cleaning equipment? Doesn't any ole mop and cleaner work?

Let's take a stroll through the garage work shop, which is usually a man's domain. Move over men, women are wielding tools and are darn good at it.

Men learned early on that "blue light special" tools broke easily, usually busting their knuckles at the same time. They promptly headed to the hardware store for Snap On, Craftsman, DeWalts, and Makitas. Why? Because busted knuckles aren't much fun and they lost half a day's work plus the cost of the tool.

> **Cleaning Quips**
>
> Thomas Jefferson once said, "I'm a great believer in luck and I find the harder I work, the more I have of it."

Most people use their cleaning tools far more frequently than they do their garage tools—exceptions noted. Yet they buy "blue light specials" and then complain that the product failed to live up to its promise.

Cheap cleaning equipment can be far more costly both financially and to our environment than a busted wrench. Just for kicks, add up the number of mops you have purchased in the past five years. Then count the number of cleaners lining your shelf. Quite a few of them, I'd venture to say. Any guess as to the cost?

The High Cost of Penny Pinching

Your budget might be tight and you might need to watch pennies. Do you realize that buying a $15 mop four times a year costs you a tidy sum of $60 a year, or $3,000 over a lifetime? Even worse, 250 mops have been tossed into the landfill.

Let's take this global. The United States has more than 70 million households. Say each buys four mops a year. Over a 10-year period, nearly three billion mops have gone into the landfill.

Now the damage hits closer to home. These mops can't be rinsed clean, so the dirt builds on the floor and ruins the sealant. You need a toxic stripper and wax to revive the floor. If that ruined floor is stone or laminate, it means replacing the floor. Flooring is one of the most toxic products in our landfills.

Dirty Words

Not only is energy used to manufacture the mops, but millions of gallons of fuel have been spent in shipping the raw materials to the manufacturer and delivering the finished goods to market.

Quality Means Speed and Dependability

Talk to a carpenter and ask him why he uses a Makita drill. He will likely reply, "With my Makita, I can sink a screw in under 5 seconds; it used to take 5 minutes with my Drill a Bit. The motors burned out so fast I kept three spares handy."

The same holds true for cleaning equipment. Good quality tools last you far longer, do the job faster, and save you a bundle in replacement costs. Don't forget the savings to our Earth.

The Buzz on Vacuums

Cheap vacuums ain't good. The motors in cheap vacuums burn out quickly, which means frequent replacements. Stores also change brands, so finding replacement bags and belts can be tricky.

With proper care, a good vacuum lasts 20+ years. Their strong motors remove more dirt. Less dirt in the carpet means less indoor pollution and carpeting that lasts longer.

Mary's Handy Hints _____

People often ask which vacuum cleaner I recommend. After wearing out nearly a dozen of them, my personal choice is a Miele Canister. My Miele is trouble free, inhaling dirt others missed. The other vacuum cleaner bags ended up with dust on the outside of the bag, which meant dust was spewing back into the air as I vacuumed. I prefer a vacuum that traps the dust.

Before beginning your search for a vacuum, read *Consumer Reports* for recommendations. Decide ahead of time which attachments are essential for your home.

Filter It Out

The filtering system in a vacuum is key. What's the point of cleaning the floor if your vacuum spews dust out the back? High-efficiency particulate air (HEPA) filters are expensive to replace, but they trap dust, which is essential for asthma sufferers. Micro-filtration systems are an improvement over filterless systems but are not as effective as a HEPA filter.

Mary's Handy Hints _____

Janitorial supply stores can be a wonderful resource for vacuums. If you don't find a residential vacuum, try a commercial vacuum. This website compares vacuums: www.allergybuyersclubshopping.com/vacuumcleaners.

Upright Vacs

Upright vacuums are easier to store than canisters. However, canisters are easier on your neck and back because the heavy vacuum is behind you. Test drive them at the store to decide which suits you. Canisters do have better suction than uprights. Plus, uprights kick debris out the back, while canisters inhale that stuff.

Canister Vacs

Canisters take up more room in the closet, but they have an automatic retrieval system for the cord—no more hand-winding cords. Plus there are no tubes to assemble when you need to use an attachment. They are easier to clean as well.

Backpack Vacs

Janitorial supply stores carry backpack vacuums. They are great in office buildings but could be tricky in a home. One quick turn to attend a child, and you just shattered a glass door.

Shopping for a Vacuum

My soapbox gets good use in this chapter because many of these products don't fess up to their promises. For instance, some manufacturers tout the lightness of their vacs—one-finger lifting!

Stop! It takes a strong motor to lift dust and dirt from deep within carpeting. Lightweight does not a powerful vacuum make. You don't need a muscle machine, but you need oomph in a motor and that does not come with a light motor.

Before purchasing a vacuum, run it up and down the aisles. Listen for any clinking or straining noises the vacuum spews at you. Take an extension cord to reach half the aisle to get a better feel for the machine. Most homes have carpet and hard floor surfaces, so take that machine for the ride of its life.

Here are other issues to consider when looking at vacuums:

◆ Does the vacuum kick dirt out the back? If so, that machine seems pretty worthless, doesn't it?

◆ Is there a manual switch to take you from carpets to a hard floor surface?

◆ Sit down and have a good look under the hood. How easy is it to remove the *beater bar* to change the belt? Is the belt a good heavy-duty belt or one that will break easily?

A **beater bar** is a rigid bar in a vacuum that agitates and loosens the dirt in a carpet.

◆ Is there dust and dirt around the beater bar? If so, then the suction is not up to snuff.

◆ Visit the websites of various vacuum cleaning companies to get a feel for what you need in a vacuum. Leave your checkbook at home to avoid being pressured into buying a machine that is not right for you. Take notes on models you like; then shop at home where you can make a pressure-free decision.

Next, look at the disposable bag. Is it worn along the seam line? Is there dust on the outside of the bag? Is there dust inside the canister that holds the bag? If so, it means the dust flies—inside your home as well as the vacuum.

Rags, Cloths, Scrubbers, and Sponges

What? Dedicate an entire section to rags and sponges in a cleaning book? Your garage is full of all kinds of rags. Some of those rags could set you back a few bucks refinishing furniture.

Read on for the pros and cons of various choices.

The Not-So-Wonderful Microfiber

Microfiber cloths are marvelous for many uses. Dampened, they remove some food stains from carpeting and are unbeatable for cleaning windows and mirrors.

Most cleaning books on the market tout the wonders of microfiber towels. A closer look at the fabric will tell you to *caveat emptor*, which is Latin for "It can wreck your furnishings." Microfiber is made from 80 percent polyester, which is plastic. Plastic scratches the sealant, finish, paint, or coating off any surface with repeated use. The scratches are very fine, so you don't notice the damage—until it's too late.

Dirty Words _____

The rule of thumb for using microfiber is if the surface is sealed, finished, or painted, do not use microfiber to clean it. This includes marble; granite; Corian; wood; laminates; and painted surfaces such as walls, cars, vehicles, boats, and airplanes.

Purchase high-quality microfiber. Cheap microfiber "ain't good." It leaves lint and falls apart in the washer.

Good Ole Dependable Cotton

Want safe? Want dependable? Then stick to 100 percent cotton rags. Frayed hand towels that lost their place in the bathroom make great rags for kitchen and bathroom duty. You can't beat them for mopping floors. Leave windows sparkling by using 100 percent cotton baby diapers or lint-free towels.

The Ultimate Dry Sponges

Nontoxic chemically treated dry sponges first made their appearance in the Jan San (janitorial sanitation) industry for removing soot from walls after a fire. They blossomed into the retail market for whisking away pet hair on furniture and dust on lampshades. Put them to work on clothing, car seats, or fabric pleated blinds.

Clean them by sanding them outside with fine grit sandpaper.

Mary's Handy Hints _____

When you clean your windows, use a dry sponge to clean the screens rather than taking hours to hose down and wash them.

Scrubbers and Brushes

You'll need several brushes (and a scrubber) to complete your cleaning chores. Here is the list:

- White nylon scrubbing pad; the colored pads scratch.

- An old toothbrush. (No, you can't use your partner's.) They nab those hard-to-reach areas like around bathrooms faucets.

- Toilet bowl brushes made either from cotton or bristles. Use a brush that does not contain metal parts, which can leave ugly scratches on the toilet and can rust.

- Kitchen brushes. Those most often used are brushes for pots and pans, sinks, and bottle brushes.

- Threaded nylon brushes that attach to a handle. They strip wax off linoleum or vinyl flooring. Use them on shower floors.

- A 1 and $^1/_2$ inch paintbrush for cleaning pleated lampshades or getting into small areas such as corners of windows.

- A ceiling fan cleaning brush.

If you only use brushes to brush your hair or teeth, get thee to a hardware store and stock up on these cleaning brushes!

Dirty Words

I found that grout cleaning brushes don't just clean grout—they remove it entirely! Use a product called The StainEraser (see Appendix B).

Sweep It with a Glance

Find yourself sweeping dirt under the rug? This section is for you. It's best to use a 100 percent cotton dust mop on hardwood, laminated, marble, or granite flooring. Steer clear of a dust mop made from microfiber for floor surfaces unless you have a couple thousand dollars extra to refinish or replace your floor.

Brooms with bristles will scratch these surfaces as well. Bristled sweeping brooms quickly scoot dirt out from the grout of tiled floors, although vacuuming is by far faster.

If you have a large area to dust, head to a janitorial supply store for an 18-inch-wide 100 percent cotton dust mop. Be sure to get an extra replacement head. They are washable and dust large areas quickly. Hold firm and use the word "no" repeatedly when they try to sell you microfiber mops.

People love their lightweight electric brooms for quick floor cleanups. They do take up closet space and are costly both to purchase and to

Mother Earth. They need replacing every 4 or 5 years and consume raw material and energy for manufacturing. Save money and our Earth by using your vacuum. Sweeping floors with a dust mop takes a few minutes longer, but arm energy is free whereas electric brooms use energy. Turn on some fast calypso music and dance the dust away with a broom or dust mop.

Mops

Shopping for a mop can be as confusing as shopping for a car. So many models! So many features! So many prices! The only thing missing is the hard-sale pitch.

Here are the pros and cons of the various kinds of mops. Mops with replaceable mop heads—sponge mops in particular—require excessive amounts of oil and energy to manufacture. The manufacturing process is hazardous to our environment, and the mops take hundreds of years to biodegrade, if they biodegrade at all.

If It's Dirty, Don't Use It

When was the last time you used a dirty wash cloth to wash your face? Ordinarily, you would use a clean wash cloth unless you are backpacking in the mountains.

You use clean wash cloths because you can't get your face clean with a dirty wash cloth. So, why are you trying to clean your floor with a dirty mop? We waste time and gallons of water trying to force dirt out of self-wringing mops and get nowhere except soaked trying to rinse them.

Yet you continue to clean your floor with a dirty mop and then wonder why your floor has dulled and feels sticky and why the mop smells from the mold.

Here are the options open to you.

Cotton String Mops

These mops work well on slate floors. Never use them on wood, laminated, linoleum, vinyl, marble, or granite floors. Not only do they hold excessive amounts of water, but the excess moisture left in them also warps the boards on wood or laminated floors and damages sealants on granite and marble. The dirt left in string mops dulls linoleum and vinyl floors.

Hang your cotton string mop outside to dry even in the dead of winter. The fibers will freeze, but they'll be dry within a few days. Ever hear of freeze-dried coffee? Many of our Canadian friends dry their clothes by hanging them outside to freeze dry.

Sponge Disasters

Sponge mops are the most energy-consuming mop to manufacture. The mop head must be replaced monthly so buy extra when you get one.

Sponges absorb moisture so they do a quick job picking up liquid spills. Spills are handled faster and more efficiently with a terry towel, micro-fiber towel, or regular sponge. Each of these requires far less energy and natural resources to manufacture.

Twist Mops

These mops actually do the twist, so put on the appropriate music. They're called *twist* mops because you twist them to wring out the water. Clean floors in sections and dry as you mop.

Cleaning Quips

"Housekeeping ain't no joke."—Louisa May Alcott

Like string and sponge mops, these heads soil quickly and must be replaced frequently so they are costly to you and the environment.

Cotton Pad Mops

Flat mops with 100 percent cotton pads can be used safely on all floor surfaces. Spritz them with water from a spray bottle until they are barely damp when mopping marble, granite, or wood floors. These easily clean under low areas such as sofas and chairs if you have hard floor surfaces throughout the home. Because they are cotton, they are safe for all floor surfaces.

Towel Mops

Towel mops use ordinary terry towels to clean the floor. They're safe for all floor surfaces because limited amounts of water remain on the towel. You can clean the towels each time you use them, so the floors aren't recontaminated with the dirt you took off them last week. Replacement costs are minimal—you use hand towels you've retired from the bathroom. They can also be used for dusting cobwebs and washing walls, ceilings, or windows.

Microfiber Mops

Microfiber mops should never be used on laminated, wood, marble, granite, or other flooring that is sealed or finished. Use extreme caution on tile or slate floors. They're unbeatable in institutional or commercial settings where the floors are continuously buffed and waxed.

Predampened Towelette Mops

Outside of the environmental issues, towelette mops pose extreme hazards to the health of your floors and the health of our Earth. The towels are so thin that they must have strong cleaners to clean the floor. The cleaners are difficult at best to rinse from a floor so the floor feels sticky. That sticky residue softens the sealant, eventually ruining the finish.

The cost to replace the towelettes is quite high, and the cost to manufacture, ship, and dispose of them is even greater. It easily takes three or four towels per cleaning. They are chemical-laden, meaning the toxins invade your home and our landfills. They can also remove the color from the edges of the carpet that butts next to the hard surface flooring. The carpet must then be redyed.

Bottle Attached Mops

People have reported that they just love the convenience of these mops. You can make your own solution for them with ¼ cup white vinegar and a teaspoon of borax per quart of water. Use only water for any kind of stone floor tile, marble, granite, or slate. Use vinegar and water only for wood or laminated floors.

Mary's Handy Hints _____

By *all-purpose cleaner*, I mean either the homemade recipe in Chapter 4 or a concentrated cleaner such as CleanEz, Bi-O-Kleen, or The Clean Team's Red Juice. See Appendix B.

Soaps and Cleaning Solutions

People spend years playing tug of war with their bottles of cleaners. They want to change to healthier products but Brand X is what Grandma always used. They use Grandma's brand because they just don't know which product to trust. They complain to me during my seminars about trying dozens of products, none of which worked.

Keep in mind that if the product you are using works and does not contain the toxins listed in Chapter 2, stick with what you are doing. But if your shower still looks gray from soap residue and the toilet displays that "ring around the collar," then it is time to beef up your cleaners.

Here is a list of the basic cleaners you need.

◆ A glass cleaner for windows and mirrors.

◆ All-purpose cleaner, which tackles toilets, showers, tubs, sinks, and kitchen counters. Use water only on granite, marble, or tile counters.

◆ A gentle scouring product such as Bon Ami, Barkeeper's Friend, or Cameo for cleaning stainless steel.

◆ All-natural organic dishwashing detergent. No phosphates are allowed because they cause a multitude of problems including mold. Many states have banned products containing phosphates.

◆ Distilled white vinegar. This wondrous product cleans everything from toilets to windows!

◆ Baking soda or washing soda for scrubbing toilets, cleaning drains, and more.

That's all you need! You noticed the list lacked toilet bowl cleaners, dusting aids, and air fresheners. They are expensive, toxic, and consume enormous amounts of energy and landfill space.

Dusters

"Dust if you must" but leave the dusters in the closet. Most dusters merely toss the dust back into the air where two days later it lands on your coffee table again. They are handy for dusting oil paintings or small figurines.

Here are a few options for you diehard duster fans.

Feather Dusters

Feather dusters are the worst of the dusters. In my testing, they leave more dust behind than their lambswool competitors. Make certain your duster is made of real ostrich feathers because the cheap, colorful, fake ones scratch furniture with plastic spines.

Lambswool is hard to beat for dusting dashboards in cars, figurines, and oil paintings. They do a great job cleaning out the ducts of your clothes dryer and furnace vents, too.

Dusting Cloths

Old but clean 100 percent cotton T-shirts, clean white cotton tube socks, or 100 percent cotton baby diapers make the best dusters. They are lint free and easily laundered.

Everyone has cotton T-shirts and tube socks that have worn out their welcome, so no further manufacturing is necessary. Use what you have at home helping to save our Mother Earth. Then use them as rags when they wear out their welcome dusting.

The Least You Need to Know

◆ Cheap or inappropriate tools can make your cleaning job difficult, time consuming, and can cost more, also.

◆ You don't need as many cleaning solutions as you think.

◆ Be sure to test and inspect vacuums thoroughly in the store to ensure that the vacuum has a strong suction.

◆ Your choice of mop depends on your floor surfaces to be cleaned.

4

MIY: Make It Yourself

In This Chapter

◆ Going green is simply simple

◆ Essential oil essentials

◆ Recipes

◆ Fresh is best

"If it's green, it's biology. If it stinks, it's chemistry. If it has numbers it's math. If it doesn't work, it's technology"—author unknown. To stir up your own cleaning concoctions, you won't need a Petri dish to grow green "stuff" or a chemistry book to decipher some foreign symbol.

This chapter teaches you step-by-step healthy ways to clean with products you make at home. Essential oils will knock your socks off with their variety of uses and how well they work. They heal sores, clean, disinfect, and deodorize to name just a few of their uses. I am not "Idiot" enough to plunge into the whole spectrum of essential oils in this book. I do pluck you into the basics for nontoxic, effective cleaning.

Check out Appendix B for ready-to-use healthy alternatives if you are not a make-it-yourselfer (MIYer).

The Basics

Now that the hairs on the back of your neck are crawling from the shock of all these toxic chemicals, here comes the fun part: recipes for ecofriendly cleaning you make at home.

Your shopping list includes the following:

- Essential oils; see the next section
- One plastic container of baking soda with holes in the lid
- One gallon distilled water—tap water does not give consistent results
- Organic liquid dish soap—the old standby liquid dish soaps are toxic and so full of fillers they barely clean dishes
- Thirty-five percent food-grade hydrogen peroxide from a health food store
- Nature's Miracle (found at most pet stores)
- Borax
- Unscented foaming shaving cream
- Lemons
- Salt
- Flour
- Spray bottles
- Olive oil

Cheap enough for you? If any of these are difficult to find, check the Yellow Pages or Appendix B.

Here are a few "essential" tips before you brew your own concoctions. Unless handled correctly, essential oils can be irritating and the results poor. Are you ready? I'm ready.

Essential Oils

Essential oils date back thousands of years. The Greek goddess Athena brought Greeks the gift of an olive tree. They used parts of it for heat, medicine, perfume, antiseptics, and food.

Suddenly life flash forwards into the twenty-first century and the value of these remarkable oils zips past us faster than my dog used to climb a tree after a cat. Even with a long history of proven results, mention "essential oils" and most people cringe as if you are a mythical wizard out of the fifteenth century.

Let's take a closer look into the marvels of these not-so-modern wonders. Essential oils are derived from plants. A distillation process removes the part of the plant that gives the plant its *essence*. This means various parts of the plant are used depending on which part contains the essence.

Rose oil comes from petals, cinnamon oil from bark, and lemon oil from the rind. Rub your hands on the pith of an orange and then smell the essence of the orange on your hands.

Mary's Handy Hints

The next time ants descend on your home, pour a few drops of Oil of Cloves along their path rather than toxic ant killer. Add small piles of cornmeal. Ants can't digest it, so they die. Use a funnel to pour cornmeal into an ant hive. This works magic on "fire" ants, which are found mostly in the south.

Essential oils are *volatile* because they evaporate readily at room temperature. An oil is *essential* in the sense that it carries a distinctive scent, or essence, of just one plant. Here are a few terms you will hear often:

- **Absolute oils.** Extracted by a solvent when steam distillation might damage the oil.

- **Aromatic chemicals.** Essential oils, each of which contains about 100 of its own combination of aromatic chemicals, giving each its own unique scent.

- **Infused oils.** Vegetable oils such as almond oil with an essential oil added to them.

♦ **Base or carrier oils.** These are always vegetable, nut, or seed oils. Essential oils are highly concentrated and must be diluted in a base oil before using them on the skin.

Some common bases include sweet almond, apricot kernel, grape seed, avocado, peanut, olive, pecan, macadamia nut, sesame, evening primrose, and walnut. Never use mineral oil or baby oil because these are petroleum products and are extremely dangerous.

> **Mary's Handy Hints**
>
> Wikipedia contains a full list of essential oils and their properties. Type en.wikipedia.org/wiki/ List_of_essential_oils into your browser. Appendix B lists sources for essential oils.

Oils possess antibacterial and antifungal functions and are excellent cleaning aids or air fresheners. The list of their uses is endless. And they work.

Know Your Stuff

If you think the odors from your son's tennis shoes are strong, take a whiff of a bottle of pure peppermint oil. Oils are highly concentrated and can irritate the skin, so care must be used when handling them.

Here are a few things to keep in mind when buying and using essential oils:

♦ *Organic*—means a farmer cannot use pesticides, weed killers, or synthetic fertilizers. To be organic, the plant or tree must be free of all chemical residues.

Buy only certified organically grown oils, including base oils. Essential oils are highly concentrated so pesticides absorbed by the plants and trees are in higher concentrations in the oil and can harm you. Rid your life of toxins; don't add to it.

♦ *Therapeutic grade* —means the oil has been extracted in such a manner as to derive as many of the fragile aromatic compounds as possible resulting in a high-grade oil. Always purchase therapeutic, cold-pressed, organic essential oils.

- Heated oils loose their potency. Cheaper, bargain oils are poor quality, are often heated, and usually contain filler oils that are not recognized base oils. Always buy cold-pressed oils.

- Store essential oils in amber or dark-colored glass bottles in the refrigerator. Be sure to place them inside airtight containers so their aromas will not affect your food. Exposure to light, oxygen, or heat causes chemical changes in the oil over time.

- Always read the precautionary statements before you use essential oils. Most websites carrying high-quality oils list the oils' adverse side effects. Read them.

Mary's Handy Hints

Some essential oil manufacturers use petroleum distillates as a filler. Distillates are carcinogenic. Place a few drops of your oil on a blotting paper. One hundred percent pure oils don't leave a residue after they've evaporated. Petroleum solvents leave a residue.

The nose knows. Smell your oils to ensure that they are fresh. Essential oils do not go rancid. However, carrier oils can go rancid and emit a rather unpleasant odor.

Oils for Cleaning and Disinfecting

When we were growing up, our folks would ground us if they ever caught us sweeping dirt under the rug to shortcut our cleaning chores. In years past, people swept sweet smelling herbs under the rug. When you walked over them, they emitted their essence and gave the room a breath of fresh air—or rather fresh herb.

Several oils not only will give your home a lift of spirit, but will clean it as well. The following is a list of the more common cleaning herbs. After this list, we give you the formulas for cleaning just about everything in your home.

Always wear gloves when working with tea tree oil or lavender because they can irritate the skin. Lemon and lime oils are far safer. Pine is one of the best oils for cleaning.

Remember that the following list of oils for cleaning does not mean you need to purchase all of them. Start with one or two of the least expensive oils to see whether you like using them. Most oils have dual uses. For instance, clove oil cleans and gets rid of pesky ants.

Most important, have fun with your oils. Choose the ones that appeal to you. Only a few drops are needed to make a cleaner so one bottle will last a year or longer if stored properly.

All these oils are excellent for cleaning:

- **Cinnamon.** Antiseptic, as well as a mind and body stimulant.

- **Clove.** Antiseptic, and repels ants.

- **Geranium.** Antiseptic, disinfectant, and cleaner. Natural insect repellent. Use as a tick repellent for dogs and humans. Add from 5 to 10 drops to carpet shampoo to repel fleas.

- **Lavender oil.** Antiseptic, antifungal, and air freshener. Repels moths, so use it in carpet shampoo for wool carpet. Use it instead of dryer sheets; see the section "Laundry Bliss," later in this chapter.

- **Lemon or lime oil.** Antibacterial, antiseptic, antifungal, and deodorizer. Excellent in cleaners, furniture polish, floor cleaner, and carpet shampoo.

- **Lemongrass.** Antiseptic, repels insects, is a good cleaning agent.

- **Orange or sweet orange oil.** This oil is listed as a warning because it is used in many cleaners. Most orange oil contains d-limonene which has been linked to cancer.

- **Oregano.** Antibacterial, antiviral, antifungal, antiseptic, anti-infectious, and antiparasitic.

- **Pine.** Cleaner, deodorizer, antibacterial, disinfectant, and antiseptic.

- **Rosemary.** Antiseptic, dishwashing liquid, deodorizer, cleaner, and wood cleaner.

- **Tea tree.** Disinfectant, antiseptic, cleaner, deodorizer, and air freshener.

- **Thyme.** Antiseptic, antibacterial, antimicrobial, disinfectant, and cleaner.

- **Verbena or lemon verbena.** Also called lemon myrtle it's an antimicrobial, a disinfectant, and a cleaner.

Dirty Words

Lavender and tea tree oil have hormone-like effects, which raises estrogen levels and lowers male sex hormones. Never apply them directly to the skin over a long period of time. Women with breast cancer should not use these oils, even in cleaners.

Recipes for the Kitchen

If I didn't carry my own line of nontoxic cleaners, the following would be the recipes I would toss together. When using a ready-made all-purpose cleaner such as my CleanEz, Bi-O-Kleen, or The Clean Team's Red Juice, you can still get a little funky with it by adding an essential oil. Pine, rosemary, or thyme are good choices. Add from 3 to 4 drops per diluted bottle.

All-purpose cleaners are used to clean areas such as showers, toilets, countertops, and appliances.

Mary's Handy Hints

When mixing your own cleaners, always use distilled water. Water qualities vary even within a town. That variation will put the kaboolz on your homemade cleaners.

All-Purpose Cleaner

Makes a 32-ounce spray bottle.

2 teaspoons borax	½ teaspoon lemon oil
4 tablespoons white vinegar	2 drops pine oil
4 cups hot water	2 drops organic liquid dish soap

Mix together in the order of the recipe, stirring until the dry ingredients dissolve. Pour into spray bottle. Do not use on Corian, granite, or marble countertops.

Corian, granite, and marble: Do not use any kind of cleaner on these countertops because it will ruin them. Mary Moppins Benya is one exception that can be used on these surfaces, or you can mix three drops of verbena essential oil in a 32-ounce bottle of distilled water. Verbena is an excellent disinfectant and does a bit of cleaning as well.

Disinfectant: First spray with 3 percent hydrogen peroxide. Do not use peroxide that is more than six months old because it will have lost its fizzle. Fill a second 32-ounce bottle with $\frac{1}{3}$ cup of distilled white vinegar; then fill it with water. Spray the surface first with the peroxide solution; then follow with the vinegar solution. Remember to mark your bottles.

Although more expensive, Nature's Miracle (found at pet stores) is an excellent alternative. I should own stock in this company for all of it I sell for them. Nature's Miracle contains enzymes that eat bacteria. Spray on the surface, wait 5 minutes, and then wipe dry. It's even safe for Corian, granite, and marble surfaces.

Floor cleaners. See Chapter 10 for specifics on floor care and cleaners.

Scouring powder. Sprinkle baking soda on the area to be scoured, and scrub it with a damp cloth. Crush an oregano leaf onto the spot for an aromatic smell and its disinfecting abilities.

Dishwasher detergent. Here is a recipe that works fairly well and costs less than 10¢ per load. NOTE: I am very hesitant to use a homemade dishwasher detergent because it might clog your dishwasher.

Dishwasher Detergent

1 cup borax	$\frac{1}{4}$ cup citric acid (available at health food stores)
1 cup baking soda	30 drops of lemon or grapefruit essential oil
$\frac{1}{4}$ cup sea salt	

You need a large bowl with a lid. Mix together the above ingredients. Shake the dry ingredients thoroughly. Place small batches in the blender and pulverize. Do not mix continuously. Pour back into the bowl, adding the essential oil. Store in a glass jar. Use one tablespoon in each dispenser cup.

Oven cleaner. Mix washing soda with organic liquid dish soap or an all-purpose cleaner such as CleanEz, Red Juice from The Clean Team, or Bi-O-Kleen and five drops of pine essential oil to form a thick paste. Plaster on the oven walls. Wait 30–60 minutes; then scrub with a dampened white scrub pad or nonabrasive pad.

Air freshener: See the section "Naturally Fresh Home," later in this chapter.

Drain opener: Most kitchen drains have disposals, and the usual remedy of baking soda and vinegar will damage a disposal. Save this combo for bathroom sinks and shower drains. To cure the kitchen drain dilemma, bring one quart of water to a boil. Turn off the stove and add one tablespoon of organic liquid dishwashing detergent. Pour this amount down each drain using a funnel to direct the water into the drain and not the sink.

Glass cleaner: In a new 32-ounce spray bottle, add 1/3 cup distilled white vinegar, 1 tablespoon organic dishwasher detergent, and 2–3 drops of verbena essential oil. Shake the bottle thoroughly until all the detergent has dissolved. Finish filling the bottle with distilled water leaving enough room to shake and mix the concoction. Eliminate the detergent should it spot the windows.

Mary's Handy Hints

Prevention is not only key to speed cleaning, but also keeps you ahead of potential problems like clogged drains. Once a month, pour a cup of Nature's Miracle down each drain before retiring for the night. The naturally occurring enzymes in Nature's Miracle eat away at the debris that generally clogs drains.

Silver polish: Put a sheet of aluminum foil into a glass bowl. Sprinkle the foil with salt and baking soda and then fill the bowl with warm water. Soak your silver in the bowl. The tarnish migrates to the foil like magic! Dry and buff.

Crystal cleaner: Use the glass cleaner recipe.

Brass: Cut a lemon in half, sprinkle it with salt, and rub the lemon on the metal. Buff with a soft cloth.

Copper: Make a paste with equal parts white vinegar, flour, and salt. Wipe it on the copper letting it set for an hour. Buff with a cloth. Tomato sauce works faster but is more expensive.

Aluminum cleaners: Scour the aluminum with a paste of calcium carbonate, organic liquid dish soap, and borax.

Bathroom Alternatives

When we hit Chapter 7, on bathrooms, pick up my handy preventive tips and I'll teach you my precision cleaning tips to zip you through the bathroom. Here is a good recipe for cleaning the shower. Or if you are like me and don't like a multitude of bottles, use the all-purpose cleaner recipe for kitchens.

Shower Cleaner

1 cup baking soda	2 tablespoons vinegar
$1/3$ cup borax	1 cup warm water
$1/2$ cup liquid soap	4 drops pine or lemon essential oil

> Mix soda, borax, and soap. Add water, mixing until the soda and borax have dissolved. Use a funnel and pour into a narrow necked bottle. Then add vinegar and oil. This recipe will bubble and fizzle just a little due to the combination of vinegar and baking soda. Pour onto a damp cloth, clean the surface, and then rinse thoroughly to avoid leaving a residue.

Bi-O-Kleen, CleanEz, or Red Juice from The Clean Team do an excellent job cleaning bathroom showers and tubs. Never purchase cleaners that come ready-to-use (RTU)) because the cost is high compared to concentrated products. Plus, RTU products mean another plastic bottle headed to the landfill. The manufacturing process to make plastics requires enormous amounts of energy.

Toilet bowl cleaner: Spray the toilet bowl with an all-purpose cleaner. Sprinkle in a bit of baking soda or borax. Wait 5 minutes and scrub with a nylon scrub brush.

Bathroom drains: Use the same technique to unclog the bathroom drain as you did for the kitchen drain. You can also pour $1/2$ cup baking soda down the drain followed by 1 cup of boiling vinegar to clear the drain. Use Nature's Miracle once a month before bed to prevent any further clogs.

Mildew remover: Mix a 50/50 solution of a 35 percent solution of food-grade hydrogen peroxide (found in health food stores) to water. Call the health food store first to be certain it is in stock. Alternatively, mix enough water with borax to form a very liquid paste, adding 5 or 6 drops of lemon oil to aid in killing the mold. Your bathroom will smell fresh, too.

Dirty Words

Never use a toilet bowl brush that contains a metal piece that holds the nylon bristles. They scratch the toilet.

Wipe or spray on the mildewed areas. Wait 30 minutes and repeat. Then wait two hours. Next, clean with straight white vinegar and let that set overnight. Do not shortcut this recipe by mixing vinegar and peroxide together. Combined, they negate each other's effectiveness as mold killers.

Healthy Dusting

Make your own furniture polish by mixing several drops of lemon essential oil together with liquid beeswax. Never use olive oil for a furniture polish or on cutting boards. It turns rancid when exposed to light, heat, and air.

Upholstery cleaner: I have always found using foaming shaving cream (gel shaving cream does not work) on upholstered furniture was the easiest way to remove stains. Liquid cleaners soak through upholstery too quickly to remove the stain and can form toxic fumes when combined with

Dirty Words

Reread Chapter 2 for warnings about linseed oil. Stay away from linseed oil in both your own homemade polish and those purchased in a store because it will spontaneously combust.

the fire retardants applied to the fabric. Foaming shaving cream sits on top, giving the product time to work.

Laundry Bliss

It is far too easy to damage a washing machine with homemade laundry detergent brews. Bi-O-Kleen and The Clean Team's Red Juice are both excellent products. Add distilled white vinegar to the wash cycle. It is an excellent cleaner and boosts the cleaning ability of your detergent, so you need less detergent. How much less? This depends on individual circumstances and water hardness. Testing is the only way to know how much to use. Start with ½ cup and add more if needed. Also add ½ cup vinegar to the rinse cycle to remove soap residue, soften the clothes, and prevent static cling. Yee haw—no more dryer sheets going into the landfill or toxic fabric softeners attacking our water supply.

Bleach: Switch to hydrogen peroxide for your laundry. Bleach turns white clothes dingy. Use borax as an alternative.

Moth repellant: To protect your fabrics, grab a cheese cloth and fill it with cedar chips, lavender leaves, eucalyptus, cinnamon sticks, or bay leaves—or any combination of these. This eliminates the need for moth balls.

Naturally Fresh Home

Spray air fresheners are expensive. The droplets linger for several days, and as you walk through the mist, you inhale them into your lungs. Plug-in air fresheners are expensive to the environment and emit toxic chemicals as do the sprays. See Chapter 16 for the lowdown on air fresheners.

Let's try a few other tricks to freshen your home naturally:

- **Buy a plant instead.** Check out Chapter 16 for plants that purify the air and add a fresh scent.

- **Use fresh lilies.** These always add a wonderful aroma to your home.

- **Plant aromatic flowers in your yard or garden that can be cut for flower arrangements.** Research gardening books for spring, summer, and fall blooming flowers so you have nearly a year-round supply.

- **Mix an essential oil with distilled water and shake to mix.** Spritz a bit onto the carpet for a refreshing, inexpensive, healthy alternative to retail room air fresheners.

- **Boil a 50/50 mixture of white vinegar to water for 10 minutes to get rid of last night's fishy odor.** Add a drop of your favorite essential oil or drop in a clove, bay leaf, slice of lemon, or bit of cinnamon for a wonderful fresh scent.

Ecofriendly Products

Companies seem to get away with making wild claims that their products are nontoxic and environmentally friendly when actually they might be just the opposite. Look for the Green Seal of Approval or other nationally recognized seals of approval.

Remember that the mere act of manufacturing any product places a burden on the environment. Look for specific information on a bottle. Does it claim to be biodegradable? If so, does it state how long it takes to biodegrade? Look for clues like "no phosphates" rather than "Earth friendly" or some other loose term.

Then check for contradictions. If it says it's biodegradable on one side of the bottle and has the toxic warnings listed in Chapter 2, then leave the product on the shelf.

Appendix B guides you to a list of Earth-friendly products.

The Least You Need to Know

- Make-it-yourself cleaners and body care products might take time, but the cost savings to you and Mother Earth are rewarding.

- Making friends with essential oils is healthy for your home and healing for you because many of them cure aches, pains, and illnesses.

- Most health food stores carry cleaners, personal body care items, as well as food in bulk, thus reducing the impact of packaging.

Chapter 5

Schedule It: Cleaning Chores, That Is

In This Chapter

◆ Why you need a cleaning schedule

◆ Create a schedule that works for you

◆ Daily and weekly to-do list

◆ The big stuff counts, too: quarterly and yearly chores

Do you remember the last time you made an appointment and showed up on time, only to find out the person you were to see was running two hours late? Or perhaps you left work in the middle of a meeting to attend your child's athletic program, only to find it was nearly over and no one told you about the time change?

Hmm … it seems like it's time to schedule a time to schedule your time. If that last sentence made sense—or even if it didn't—follow me into this world of scheduling. You might get so good at setting schedules that you'll turn it into a paid hobby. This chapter teaches you how to meld cleaning into your daily life so it becomes second nature.

The Scheduling Countdown

A cleaning schedule isn't like a pair of one-size-fits-all tights. Everyone's home varies in its layout, size, number of floors, and doo-dads. Before plotting a cleaning schedule, survey the interior and exterior of your home *and take notes* on these:

◆ **All areas that need cleaning.** This one's simple: If you see it, you need to clean it. Scan each room from top to bottom making note of everything from furniture to ceiling fans.

◆ **Items that can be stored behind glass.** Tiny, decorative objects take considerable time to clean. If you can, put them behind a glass cabinet and clean them four times a year; it's better than weekly.

◆ **How frequently you need to clean each room.** If used infrequently, rooms like a formal living, dining room, and spare bedrooms might need only a monthly cleaning. Rotate them on a weekly cleaning schedule so that each room is cleaned once a month, leaving time to clean other things like baseboards.

Handing Out Tasks

With notes in hand, create a schedule (we give you a sample later in the chapter). Take into account what needs cleaning and when. Include family members if they are present in your home; keep in mind children's ages and abilities.

Okay, now where do you start? Start by remembering there is no right or wrong way to set a cleaning schedule. Simply stick to the schedule you set. It will change as children grow and circumstances change. Before you bring family members together for chore assignments, though, organize the cleaning list you made.

If you are a two-member household, weekly chores will include vacuuming, damp mopping, and kitchen duty. The dusting and bathrooms can squeak by with twice-monthly cleanings. Alternate chores weekly among family members, especially pet care, so one person isn't stuck scooping poop for the entire month.

Naming Names

Everyone should help with chores whether they are children, spouses, roommates, or parents and adult children who have moved back in with you. When you are ready to talk to the household about chores, don't approach them in a meek manner. Firmly but kindly express that the chores will be done, on time. Any hesitation on your part sends a clear message that you don't mean what you say. Your directives will be ignored.

Make this fun by gathering everyone around the table and perhaps playing a board or card game. The winner gets first choice as to the chores he will do for the week (this needs to be consistent with the above where I mentioned switching jobs weekly); keep going down the line. Perhaps the next week the loser selects the chores the winner does for that week. Get creative, but have fun.

Mary's Handy Hints

As soon as a child is steadily walking, he is old enough to put away toys. Start a child young. It pays off with less whining in later years. Lavish the praise and remember that kids are *not* little adults and will not accomplish a job like an adult.

Little Green Cleaners: Getting Kids to Help

Children are like baby ducks: lead, they follow. You can't expect them to pick up their room, set the table, or help with dinner when the house is cluttered and needs cleaning and dinner is always late.

Young children won't do things to your expectations. A one-year-old will miss the toy box. At two, the toy won't go in neatly, but by three, most kids can master neatness. Encourage them with praise like, "Wow, you got the teddy bear in the box—way to go." Kids of all ages stop helping if they are criticized.

Reward them with personal time with you, not with money. Keep the allowance out of it. A lot of people will object. Children are a part of the family, and each member should contribute. They can be paid for chores beyond their weekly chores if they want to earn extra money. An allowance is a set amount each week whether they get their chores done or not.

What happens if the child does not do his chores? You have to do the chore for him, which means you no longer have time to take him to practice or accomplish other necessary tasks. Turn the TV and computer off and make sure your child doesn't go anywhere until chores and homework are finished.

It's called responsibility. If your child misses practice because he didn't get his chores or homework done, then he sits out the next game. It won't happen again. Giving in even once means you lose face and will be pushed to the limit forever after.

Dirty Words

Watch what you say around your children. If you express your displeasure toward housework, guess what attitude your children will have? Get rid of the "stinkin' thinkin'."

Even two-year-olds can clear their plates and take them to the kitchen. Say, "Julie, I'm taking my plate to the kitchen. Bring yours and we'll rinse it off." Kids love to play in water, so have them pull a stool up to the sink and rinse off the dishes.

Not sure which task to schedule when? Read on for the breakdown of when and why you do what.

Daily Duties

Each day you face a dozen little tasks that require only a few minutes of time. Those few minutes are key to keeping your home from becoming a disaster. You can spend a few minutes now cleaning or hours later after the dirt builds up:

- Put things away as you finish using them. Promising to put it away later equals clutter. Promise one thing—put it away now.

- Air the beds. You sweat during the night, especially with "night sweats." Throw back the sheets and air the bed while you shower.

- Make the beds. Isn't it nice to come home to a neatly made bed? Also, remember that your children copy your example so give them good ones to follow.

◆ Rinse the dishes and put them in the dishwasher after every meal. Each family member should do her own dishes. My father had a rule in our home about catching fish. "You catch it, you clean it, you cook it, you eat it." You eat off it, you clean it.

◆ Keep a spray bottle of an all-purpose cleaner under the sink, along with a clean rag. Spray any spills on the stove immediately. Let it set while you eat; then wipe it away. Easy!

Mary's Handy Hints

Refill your spray bottles that holds your cleaner after you finish cleaning. Then if a spill arises, the bottle is ready for fast action.

◆ Each night clean one additional kitchen surface, such as a countertop or the microwave. By the end of the week, the kitchen will be clean with it taking you only two or three minutes per night.

◆ Start a load of laundry right before you make dinner. Before you put dinner on the table, your clothes will be ready to put in the dryer. The clothes will then be dry by the time dinner ends.

◆ If your household includes dogs, cats, or rambunctious 12-year-olds, keep fur and dirt under control with daily vacuuming.

◆ At the end of every day, tear out of the paper any articles or coupons you need and toss the rest, along with junk mail, into the recycle bin.

The idea behind daily chores is to get a simple task out of the way so you don't shudder and say, "Oh, I meant to do that yesterday." Keeping ahead of these little things means you don't need toxic cleaners for scrubbing the tough stuff.

Weekly Work

As you read this chapter, the more involved chores need to be done less and less frequently. Weekly chores are heavier than daily chores. Monthly chores are heavier still. By the time you get to yearly chores, we'll have you pushing boulders up hills!

As you look over the schedule, you might need to shift weekly chores to every other week. You might need to clean bathrooms or dust only every other week. If so, then schedule the dusting for one week and the bathrooms for the next:

◆ Change and launder sheets and pillowcases. We discuss laundry in Chapter 14.

◆ Go through the refrigerator and toss anything that smells bad. We cover kitchen cleaning in Chapter 6.

◆ Get a clean damp cloth, squirt it with a bit of liquid dish soap, and wipe around cabinet handles. Oil from your hands quickly deteriorates most sealants, so cleaning the cabinet handles weekly can eliminate the need for an expensive refinishing job.

Dirty Words

Use microfiber on glass only. Microfiber has been touted as a miracle cloth, but it's 80 percent polyester or plastic. Microfiber cleans with water only because plastic scratches the dirt off the surface. Because it doesn't know where the dirt ends and the sealant, finish, or paint begins, over time, it removes the sealant from any surface, including walls, furniture, vehicles, and flooring.

◆ Add kitchens to your weekly to-do list. Do this if you don't clean sections of the kitchen nightly, as we recommended in the "Daily Duties" section. Follow the instructions in Chapter 6.

◆ Even if you don't need to clean your bathrooms every week, spot clean the toilet and counter. See Chapter 7.

◆ If you live in a dusty area like a desert, weekly dusting is a must. Sand and dust accumulate in the grains of wood, drying and cracking it. Regular care keeps it in tip-top shape.

◆ Sweep and damp-mop hard floor surfaces. Instructions for floor care are included in Chapter 10.

◆ Clean the blinds or day/night shades in one or two rooms each week depending on the number of blinds in your home.

◆ Vacuum at least the main traffic areas weekly.

Some people prefer to scatter jobs throughout the week rather than cram them into one day. If you fit this description, decide which day you'll dust, clean bathrooms, vacuum, and damp-mop the floors; then stick to that schedule.

Mary's Handy Hints

Here's a tip for cleaning those pesky Venetian blinds: barely dampen an old sock, put it over your hand, and run your socked hand over the slats.

Twice Is Nice

You need to do these tasks every other week to keep your home in tip-top shape:

- Clean the bathrooms following the instructions in Chapter 7.

- If you can get by with dusting every other week, consider alternating dusting one week with bathroom cleaning the next.

- Thoroughly vacuum the carpet. See Chapter 10.

- Clean the drip pans on your stove and the stove hood.

- Don't forget the formal rooms and spare bedrooms.

It's easy to push twice-monthly tasks off for another time. Keep on schedule with them. Pushing them back only allows these less-frequent projects to build on top of each other. Then you'll feel stressed because you have so much work to do.

Monthly Missions

Some of these tasks are ones you might not normally think of until they go undone for so long that you *have* to notice them:

- Sweep the garage, patio, sidewalks, and other outdoor areas.

- Clean patio furniture during the months it is in use.

- Dust the cobwebs inside the house.

- Wipe down baseboards, doors, and doorways in two rooms of the house. This way, the entire home is cleaned twice a year.

◆ Change or clean furnace filters if the air conditioner or furnace is running. Do this once per quarter in off seasons.

◆ Pour an organic enzyme product such as Nature's Miracle (found in pet stores) down each drain at night before retiring. It contains enzymes that eat the gunk in your drain. Plus, it's healthy for the environment because it eats nasty bacteria in the sewers.

◆ Wipe off fabric furniture using a dry sponge.

◆ Dust wall hangings.

As I've gotten older, it has become easier to spread chores out a bit so they don't seem so overwhelming. So tackle two of these chores every week or gather the clan for an all-day marathon. When my son was young and we did the marathon, he got to choose a family outing after the cleaning was done.

Dirty Words

Sweep your driveway rather than using precious water to hose it down. Hosing takes far more time than you would spend hanging onto the end of a broom. Gather the kids, have a ball, and get some exercise by raking and sweeping.

One Quarter at a Time

If you are like me and find it hard to remember to schedule quarterly cleaning tasks, then let the change of the seasons be your reminder. Otherwise, mark you calendar for January, April, July, and October:

◆ Clean kitchen and bathroom cabinets with a cleaner made especially for wood.

◆ Remove cobwebs from the eaves of the house. You can use a broom to bat them away and end up with cobweb hair, or you can grab a mop with an extension handle and an old terrycloth towel. Extend the handle, toss the towel over the mop head, and have at the cobwebs. Cobwebs will stick to your towel rather than your hair.

- Wipe down walls for fingerprints using CleanEz or Red Juice from The Clean Team. Never use dish soap because it leaves a residue that will gum up the paint the next time you paint.

- Clean windows whenever they look dirty or the stars are no longer visible on a clear night.

- Light fixtures should be cleaned at least twice a year, and quarterly if you live in a dusty area. Some light fixtures are attached with hinges. Spritz a lint-free cloth with your cleaner and wipe it over the glass. Use a second dry cloth to dry it. Loosen the hinge, drop the glass, and do the other side.

- Vacuum and clean refrigerator coils and filters. See Chapter 6 for details on cleaning.

- Clean ceiling fans. See Chapter 11 for details.

- Remove the contents of one section of your kitchen cabinets. Toss anything unused, past the expiration date, or that you don't remember when you bought it. Clean the shelves.

- Clean hanging chandeliers. Most lighting shops carry a spray to clean the baubles without removing them. Cover furniture with plastic and place towels on top to catch drips.

 Mary's Handy Hints

Stay focused on the chore at hand. Cleaning is not the time to multitask. You build speed as you clean. Every time you stop to deal with the laundry or another chore, it takes time to get back up to speed.

Yearly Yowls

Great things happen annually: holidays, your birthday, your anniversary—and these special cleaning chores:

- Twice a year, at the beginning of summer and winter, replace the filters in your forced-air heating system.

Mary's Handy Hints

Use a wet or dry vac to clean the dryer hose. The extension tube reaches the length of the hose.

- Clean the lint out of your dryer vent every six months to prevent fires and increase the dryer's efficiency. Detach the duct that leads outside the house and clean the vent with a brush or rag.

- Have your furnace ducts cleaned professionally.

- Check for mold in bathrooms and treat it if necessary by cleaning with 35 percent food-grade hydrogen peroxide.

- Move all heavy furniture to clean behind and underneath it.

- Clean your closets.

If time is tight, don't hesitate to skip a weekly cleaning to attend to these important but time-consuming tasks.

The Least You Need to Know

- Cleaning schedules should run fuss-free like they are second nature.

- Speak positively about keeping a clean home so it is fun for the family.

- Prevention is key, so attend to the daily tasks.

- Keep a cleaning calendar going so you know who is on first and what is on second.

Part 2

Room-by-Room Cleaning Guide

A room is a room is a room—whip out some ol' cleaner and a rag and just get the job done. Right? Not quite. Each room has its own challenges and individual cleaning needs. From the kitchen where your shiny stainless steel dulls with oily fingerprints, to the bathrooms where the "throne" may not be so royal. We'll help you meet the challenge of cleaning each room using nontoxic cleaners and safe tools.

Chapter 6

Kitchen Duty

In This Chapter

- ◆ Attacking the germs in your kitchen
- ◆ Scouring sinks, drains, and garbage disposals
- ◆ Cleaning the big stuff
- ◆ Speaking of cookware

"Build it and they will come." Just as in the movie *Field of Dreams*, we do a lot of our dreaming in the kitchen sipping on a cup of tea. The family also gathers in the kitchen to plan the week, talk about the day's happenings, laugh, and oh yeah, eat.

Family members are not the only ones drawn to the kitchen. Germs, bacteria, ants, roaches, and spiders invade this space in droves. Bacteria growth explodes on any morsel of food. You don't need a magnifying glass to find out what invaded the once-white-but-now-turned-green sauce in the back of the fridge.

This chapter preps you in the art of cleaning and disinfecting every surface in your kitchen au natural. No disease-causing chemicals allowed. Put the kibosh on those germs without turning your home and your body into a toxic waste dump.

Alive in Your Kitchen

This is another chapter where I turn all serious. To wit: The Centers for Disease Control and Prevention estimates that 76 million Americans get sick; more than 300,000 are hospitalized; and 5,000 die from food-borne illnesses each year. Children are the most at risk then the elderly, people with compromised immune systems, and pregnant women.

At home, we lose the battle against viruses and bacteria by not washing our hands, undercooking food, leaving food sit out, and allowing meat juice to drip on counters or cutting boards. The germs cause nausea, diarrhea, abdominal cramping, fever, and sometimes bloody stools. Here are some of the little bugs that might be living in your food and your kitchen:

- **Shigellosis.** Lurks in milk, dairy products, and poultry. Dirty hands and undercooked foods cause these bugs to multiply in your food.

- **Campylobacteriosis bacteria.** Are found in poultry, cattle, and sheep. The chief sources are raw poultry, meat, and unpasteurized milk.

- **Listeriosis.** Hides out in soft cheese, unpasteurized milk, imported seafood products, frozen cooked crab meat, cooked shrimp, and imitation shellfish. Heat does not kill it.

 **Mary's Handy Hints** _____

Learn more about food-borne illnesses and prevention at these websites: Fight Bac! (www. fightbac.org), The Centers for Disease Control and Prevention (www.cdc.gov/health/foodill.htm), and Government Food Safety (www.foodsafety.gov).

Now that you have the idea, let's green your kitchen using nontoxic methods and roust the buggers out of their hiding places.

Sink Secrets

The kitchen sink rules the roost when it comes to contaminated kitchen surfaces. From dirty dishes to filling the dog's dish to pouring sour food into the disposal, the sink does double duty absorbing every imaginable germ in the house.

You'd better sit down for this one: according to a University of Arizona microbiologist, there is more fecal matter in your kitchen sink than in your toilet. After cleaning the sink, wipe it with a 50/50 solution of white vinegar to water followed by hydrogen peroxide—the ecofriendly way to disinfect.

If you need to bathe your baby or pet in the sink, clean the sink afterwards as instructed previously. Their little bottoms are precious but their fecal matter does not belong in your sink. Follow me to shiny, germ-free sinks.

Stainless Steel

Stainless-steel sinks tend to spot or rust. Grab a handful of baking soda, a squirt of liquid dish soap, a bit of hot water, and a brush. Scrub and then dry, which prevents rust and water marks.

When stubborn water marks get your dander riled, lay an old dish cloth on top of the marks and saturate it with white vinegar. Scrub it with baking soda. Then remove the rust with fresh-squeezed lemon juice and salt.

Cast Iron and Porcelain

These sinks stain easily so don't leave dirty dishes sitting in them. Trust me, you will attempt to banish a stain one time and never again leave dishes in the sink. Use a soft cloth to dry the sink after each use; otherwise, the water spots will wink at you and won't come out.

Do *not* use microfiber to dry or clean any sink. Made from 80–85 percent polyester, which is plastic, these cloths will eventually scratch the sealant off any surface.

Mary's Handy Hints

Use rinse baskets and sink mats to protect porcelain and cast-iron sinks.

Mix a paste of hydrogen peroxide and baking soda, and then rub the sink gently with a soft cloth to remove stains. Steel wool and abrasive sponge pads are on my hit list of things not to use on a sink. Clean a cast-iron sink regularly with liquid dish soap.

Vitreous China and Fireclay

Dry vitreous china and fireclay sinks after each use like you do cast iron. A bit of liquid dishwashing detergent does a good job cleaning them. Use caution with abrasive cleaners because they will scratch. Borax can be used occasionally if it's dissolved first.

Composite, Acrylic, Quartz, Marble, and Granite

Do not set hot pans, dishes containing acidic food such as tomato sauce, or tea or coffee cups directly on these sinks because they stain easily and acids etch the surface. Clean these sinks frequently with a mild detergent. Mix a paste of hydrogen peroxide and baking soda to remove stains.

Corian

That hot tomato salsa sure spiced up your taste buds, but it left stains on your Corian sink. Rinse dishes thoroughly before setting them in a Corian sink.

Remove stains by first soaking them with hydrogen peroxide as you do with composite sinks. Scrub with a bit of baking soda after the peroxide has set for 15–20 minutes.

Mary's Handy Hints

Clean sink stoppers and rubber sink mats by soaking them in hot sudsy water for an hour, adding $\frac{1}{4}$ cup of borax. Scrub with a scrub brush or white scrub pad.

Prevent Gunky Drains

After pouring grease, oil, food scraps, and who knows what else down our drains, little wonder they clog and smell. When they do clog, people often turn to drain openers that contain toxic chemicals like lye, sodium hydroxide, and sodium hypochlorite.

Here are safe alternatives for smooth-flowing drains:

◆ Mix a cup of white vinegar, $1/2$ cup of water, and two tablespoons of salt in a pan; bring it to a boil. Turn off the heat, and add two tablespoons of liquid dish soap. Pour this down the drain, wait 30 minutes, and then flush with plenty of hot water.

◆ Once a month, pour two cups of Nature's Miracle (found at pet stores) down each drain (if you have a dual sink) before going to bed. The enzymes eat any food in the drain.

Never use baking soda and vinegar to clear stuck kitchen drains. This combo works well in other drains, but don't dump it down your disposal. The baking soda jams the blades, damaging the motor. Debra Lynn Dadd, author of *Home Safe Home* recommends using fine mesh strainers in drain openings to prevent clogs.

What Do You Mean, Clean My Garbage Disposal?

You put garbage down your disposal, so of course it's going to smell. Here are a few easy cleaning tips:

◆ Toss a few ice cubes into the disposal while it's running. This scours the blades.

◆ Run two or three lemon peels through the disposal along with the ice chips to freshen the drains.

◆ A curved bottle brush swiftly cleans the sides of a disposal. Pour on a bit of liquid dish soap and then scrub away. Follow with the previously mentioned lemon peels and ice cubes; in less than two minutes, your disposal will smell fresher than a bouquet of roses. Okay, that is stretching things a bit, but the improved aroma will meet with your nose's approval.

Appliance Wonders

More appliances end up at Goodwill due to a lack of care than any other reason. Remember the saying "Good ain't cheap and cheap ain't good"? When it comes time to purchase new kitchen appliances, buy the best quality you can afford.

Caring for Stainless Steel

There is a placket in a small South Dakota store that reads "Menopause: It's the only time of my life I've ever been called a hot mama."

There are other things that can be "hot" as well—like new trends in clothing or household appliances. The current trend in appliances is stainless steel. It is beautiful as well as durable, but fingerprints and dulled surfaces can get you sweating like a menopausal moment.

Take a deep breath because a simple solution is at your fingertips. The secret to keeping stainless steel looking new is weekly cleaning. Dirt builds in the grain of stainless steel, dulling the surface, so always rub with the grain. Clean stainless steel appliances once a week using undiluted white vinegar. Heat stains on stoves and ovens usually scrub off with club soda.

Dirty Words

Never use chlorine bleach on stainless steel; in fact, for your health's sake stop using it altogether. Avoid abrasives, including microfiber, which will scratch. Use 100 percent terry cloth towels.

Various organic stainless steel cleaners and polishes are available. One can be found at www.ecoprocote.com. It carries the U.S. Environmental Protection Agency approval and is Earth friendly.

It's Hot—The Stove, That Is

If you're lucky enough to have a self-cleaning oven, follow its directions. Lock the door, turn on the self-cleaner, and it's off to the races! Cleaners of any kind damage self-cleaning or continuous-cleaning ovens. Do not use them on these ovens.

All other ovens must be cleaned the old-fashioned way: manually. Regardless of whether you are using green cleaners, open windows. Turn on the stove fan and wear a mask, gloves, and old clothes. Place plastic on the floor followed by several layers of newspapers to protect the floor surface.

Make a paste of baking soda and a concentrated organic cleaner like CleanEz or Bi-O-Kleen. Paste it onto the oven's surfaces and let it sit for a couple of hours. Scrub with a white scrub pad. Repeat if needed, and then rinse with white vinegar and water.

Baby you are cookin' and the top of the stove proves it. Clean light messes with detergent, water, and a little elbow grease. Lay a dish rag with really hot water and liquid dish soap on top of those splatters. It softens them as you eat dinner.

> **Dirty Words**
>
> Sprinkle salt on oven spills when the oven is still hot. The gunk will come right up after the oven cools.

A plastic scraper comes in handy to remove stubborn spots, or try a baking soda paste. Easy does it with the scraper, though, because stoves scratch easily. This might sound strange, but rub the spot with non-gel toothpaste. Sometimes it works.

We all ignore the underside of the stove hood for as long as possible. Wipe down that area weekly with a cloth dampened in very hot sudsy water so it's not such a chore. Boil some water on the back burner to soften the gunk.

For tougher grease buildup, bring $1/4$ cup white vinegar to a boil. Remove it from the heat and add enough baking soda to make a paste. Squirt in 1 drop of liquid dish soap and stir to mix. Place an old towel on top of the stove; then paste the mixture underneath the hood and wait 15 minutes. Rinse thoroughly.

Dishin' the Dirt on Fridges and Freezers

When the snack monster strikes, we all reach for the refrigerator door hoping some tasty tidbit will quiet our growling stomach. The snack you want is, of course, at the back of the shelf and you just knocked over the mustard jar reaching for it. Go ahead and laugh. I'm not known for my neatness in the kitchen.

The inside of a refrigerator is a mini-circus with various "acts" going on at one time. Act one: spills happen and when one food spills on another, bacteria begins to grow. Act two: foods also share odors. Your milk can end up smelling like fried onion rings. Prevent all these problems and keep ahead of food turning moldy by cleaning your fridge weekly.

I'd rather dig dandelions than spend an hour cleaning out the refrigerator. Time-consuming as it may be, though, it is important to keep it clean. If food turns rancid, getting rid of that smell is harder than getting rid of dandelions.

Mary's Handy Hints

The night before you do your weekly grocery shopping, clean the refrigerator after dinner, but before putting away leftovers. The fridge is nearly empty so cleaning is a breeze. Make your grocery list as you clean. Wow, talk about multitasking!

Mary's Handy Hints

Be sure to use warm, not hot, water to wash glass shelves because hot water can crack them. Add $\frac{1}{2}$ cup of white vinegar to the water for sparkling shelves.

If you are like me and just can't find the time to clean the entire refrigerator all at once, clean the shelves one week and the drawers and door shelves the next. I find dividing time-consuming chores into chunks gets them done rather than ignored.

Here is a quick way to clean the fridge. Remove large items on a shelf, tossing out items that are going green on you. Shove everything to one side. Wash the shelf, sides, and back of the fridge with warm soapy water; dry and then repeat on the other side moving older food to the front to eat immediately.

A cloth dampened with white vinegar kills mildew and removes bad odors. Sprinkle a bit of borax onto the vinegar towel for an extra cleaning boost.

Vacuum condenser coils twice a year to prevent damaging the motor. Clean coils use less energy, extending the life of the motor and saving energy. Read your directions first. A curved bottle brush reaches the deeper parts of the coil, but be careful not to snag the wires.

The makers of our refrigerator placed the coils along the bottom of the fridge. Metal panels on all four sides block access to them. We have to rent an air compressor to blow out the dust. Check the accessibility of the coils when buying a new refrigerator.

Save Water, Run Your Dishwasher

Oh, you've heard the debate—dishwasher versus hand washing. Dishwashers use far less water than hand washing. The small amount of electricity they use pales in comparison to what it takes to heat water for hand washing. When it comes to saving our planet, less is best. Here is a closer view on dishwashers.

Dishes not coming out clean? Chlorine in the water can deteriorate the water inlet valve, which then fails to provide enough H_2O to clean the dishes. Start the machine and open it after it has filled. The water on the bottom should touch the sides. If not, follow the manufacturer's directions and replace the inlet valve.

Chlorine causes far more serious problems than just clogging the inlet valve. When you open the door, what you smell is toxic, volatized chlorine—from the water and your detergent. After running your dishwasher, open the window before you open the dishwasher's door. Then switch to an organic detergent to eliminate most of the toxins.

Mary's Handy Hints

To make cleaning easier, smart cooks (like yourself!) clean as they go. Make sure the dishwasher is empty so you can load dishes as you dirty them. Start your pans soaking or even clean them while you wait for dinner to cook.

Counter Encounters

Use your own homemade cleaner or an Earth-friendly cleaner and a cotton terrycloth towel (not microfiber) to clean counters. Keep all cleaners off granite, marble, or stone countertops unless you like ugly pits in them. Clean stone countertops with hot water only. Disinfect them with Nature's Miracle, which has been previously discussed.

Cabinet Caboodle

Cabinets are the most expensive items in your kitchen, yet no one tells you how to care for them. Let's fix that.

Don't use microfiber cloths to clean cabinets or wood furniture; it scratches and will eventually strip the sealant or finish off any surface, including your vehicles. Use clean, 100 percent cotton towels for cleaning all surfaces.

Clean cabinets located above the stove and below the sink weekly. Also clean all door knobs weekly. Dust them with a barely damp cloth once a month.

Do your research when selecting a wood cleaner or conditioner for your cabinets or wood furniture. Chapter 2 warns you of the dangerous chemicals contained in some wood care products.

Experts advise against using products made from wax because it can ruin the finish. Natural beeswax does not build up on a surface. Artificial waxes will. The culprit behind cabinet damage is the petroleum distillates some products add to wax. Distillates soften the finish causing it to feel gummy and look dull.

Way back in yonder years, cabinets came in one finish: lacquer. Now there are various beautiful finishes. That's the good news. The not-so-good news is that each finish requires a different treatment. Let's learn the right way to clean these finishes.

Whitewashed and Painted Cabinets

Clean whitewashed and painted cabinets with soap, warm water, and a soft cloth. Wood treatments do not penetrate through paint so don't waste your time or money treating them. Wood must be conditioned to prevent drying and cracking. You might want to think twice before painting cabinets or buying painted cabinets.

Acrylic

These finishes are popular in the RV industry and are gaining popularity in the home. They look like they have 50 layers of a polyurethane finish on them and are gorgeous. Acrylic-finished cabinets cannot be treated with a wood conditioner.

Use only 100 percent cotton towels to clean them. Oil from your hands or cooking damages the finish. Clean them weekly, particularly around the door knobs to prevent deterioration of the finish. Do not apply polish or wax, and never use microfiber on them.

Tung Oil and Baked Finishes

Most cabinets have a baked finish, a light glossy look. These cabinets need monthly dusting with a barely damp cotton cloth. Clean around door knobs weekly with warm soapy water.

Condition them twice a year with wood conditioner; otherwise, the wood may dry and crack. Do not use conditioners or treatments containing petroleum distillates. See the previous warning.

Veneer

Whew, just one more to go. Get out that cotton dust cloth and make time for veneer cabinets once a month. Yes, I heard those groans—sorry. Dust penetrates into the grooves and will damage them quickly. Treat them as you would tung oil finishes. Veneer cabinets require conditioning at least twice a year to prevent drying and cracking. Double that if you live in a dry climate.

Cookware and You

We all bite off more than we can chew at times. Depending on the cookware and bakeware you use, you might unwittingly be doing just that. Other than the food you eat, the cookware you use has a tremendous impact on your long-term health.

It is well known that aluminum cookware seeps aluminum into your food. Coated cookware? Those chunks of coating that scrape into your food are toxic to your body. Underneath that coating is aluminum.

And I've read the rants about cast-iron cookware. Those pans start out silver and a year later are black from absorbing food and oil. I refuse to eat chicken fat I fried 10 years ago. Yes, heat supposedly kills the bacteria, but I'll pass.

Good cookware should be durable and transmit energy from the heat source evenly across the pan or skillet. This is no easy feat when your stove is electric with round elements. You end up with heat rings on a grilled sandwich.

Cookware companies talk about *thermal conductivity* and *heat capacity*. Thermal conductivity is how quickly the pan heats up. The higher the quality cookware, the faster it heats so it reduces energy usage.

Heat capacity refers to how evenly the pan conducts heat over the entire surface of the pan. The better the capacity, the more evenly the food will cook. This means the outer edges of your hamburger are not frozen while the middle is burnt.

Here are specifics of the more popular cookware.

Mary's Handy Hints _____

People also ask me what kind of cookware I use because they know I study diet, nutrition, and cookware due to health issues. With all my research, stainless steel is by far the safest and best to use. Stainless steel by itself flunks thermal conductivity and heat capacity tests. The best stainless steel cookware has layers of aluminum and cast iron covered with several layers of stainless steel. Stainless steel tests negative for reactivity so your body does not absorb the metal.

Cast Iron

Cast iron withstands high temperatures, making it ideal for frying. Be confident that your famous chili will turn out even better with the cast iron heat retention and diffusion abilities.

Some cast iron comes preseasoned. If not, then a protective wax coating is applied to prevent rust and must be removed before seasoning. Scour the pan thoroughly. Cast iron must be seasoned to prevent rust and provide a nonstick surface. Clean it and then apply vegetable oil. Finish by heating the pan so it absorbs the oil. Clean cast iron with mild detergent and reoil it before storing to prevent rust.

Cooking experts say you can get some of your daily iron from the skillets. Yuk. Take the healthy road and get your iron from the food you eat, like beans, and not a bacteria-laden iron pan.

Be very aware of your daily iron intake if you take multiple vitamins with iron. People with liver or kidney problems should never use cast iron. Too much iron in the body decreases calcium absorption, making for brittle and easily broken bones.

Copper

Like the conductor of a world-renowned orchestra, copper is the top of the charts when it comes to conducting heat. It is unbeatable for delicate sauces or foods requiring precisely controlled temperatures.

However, the Food and Drug Administration (FDA) warns against cooking with unlined copper. The metal easily dissolves into foods. In sufficient quantities, it can cause nausea, vomiting, and diarrhea.

If you choose copper cookware, make certain it has a stainless steel lining on the inside of the pans. Then enjoy the treasures copper cookware has to offer your kitchen. Clean with sudsy water. Use a copper cleaner to remove tarnish.

Coated Cookware Beware

Slick-coated veins anyone? No? Then you might want to avoid coated cookware. Random studies have shown that 95 percent of those tested who use coated cookware have detectable levels of Teflon-related chemicals in their blood. It comes from the coating that scrapes off during cooking.

Although the heat must be high, this cookware also emits toxic fumes. The off-gassed chemicals from Teflon are persistent in the environment. They never go away, building up in your body.

Clean coated cookware with hot soapy water. Replace your cookware every three years. Don't wait until it begins to peel off because it might come off in small chucks that you don't see.

Stainless Steel

Hands down, stainless steel cookware is by far the most durable of all cookware. The finish simply won't corrode or tarnish like some cookware. The surface is nonporous and tough so it stands the test of time. I've had my original stainless steel cookware for 36 years and use it everyday. The Cookware Manufacturers' Association reports that the nickel, molybdenum, or titanium contained in stainless steel cookware prevents scratching and corrosion.

If you purchase stainless steel cookware, make sure it has cast iron sides and either a copper or aluminum bottom for maximum heat capacity and conductivity. Stainless steel by itself is a disappointing conductor of heat.

After frying food, simply put hot water in the pan, cover it with a lid, and enjoy your meal. Food stuck on the pan will then wash right off.

The Least You Need to Know

- Keep the kitchen as clean as possible because it can have more germs than your bathroom.

- Many of the appliances in your kitchen can safely be cleaned with common items in your cupboards, like vinegar.

- Keep KP duty to a minimum by cleaning as you cook.

- Choosing your cookware carefully will bring decades of excellent wear.

Chapter 7

Bathroom Blitz

In This Chapter

- ◆ Eliminate germs in your bathroom
- ◆ Keep a tidy bowl
- ◆ Scrub the tub
- ◆ Clean grout and tile

The god of annoying things strikes the hardest when it comes to the royal throne—the toilet, that is. The bathroom reigns as the most dreaded cleaning challenge in a home. Follow my preventive tips and these annoying gods will steer clear of your home.

Articles on green cleaning warn about the health problems bathroom germs cause. These articles totally miss the most toxic parts of the bathroom: water flowing from your shower and air fresheners. They are far more harmful than germs in the toilet.

No need to reach for a gas mask. Tips in this chapter lay out a battle plan that's easy to follow. You'll gain important insight into the deadly danger coming from your shower and preventive methods that you can implement immediately.

A Breath of Fresh Air ... or Not

Oh, the smells and odors escaping from the bathroom have you reaching for the can of air freshener. Hopefully in Chapter 16, you'll learn enough about the phthalates in air fresheners that you'll take yours to the toxic dump. Repeated use of these sprays causes far more severe and long-term health issues than the few germs on your bathroom faucets.

> **Dirty Words**
>
> If you or any member of your family has consistently foul-smelling stools or gas requiring an air freshener, it could be due to an undiagnosed disease like celiac sprue, which is intolerance to the gluten found in wheat, rye, and barley. Look seriously at your diet. It could be what you are eating. Do some research, change your diet, and then toss the can of air freshener. It can cause grave illnesses such as cancer.

Healthy hygienic measures such as hand washing, along with a good immune system (yes, healthy diet), allow you to throw a one-two punch to most bathroom germs. Put your phobia about bathroom germs to rest. A toilet seat is not a common transmitter of germs because germs live for only about an hour.

Besides, you must come into contact with a large quantity of germs to become infected. Thorough hand washing solves these bathroom germ contaminations.

Mold: You read correctly. Germs are not the major issue in the bathroom. Mold and mildew cause far more serious health issues. Mold multiplies in damp places, causing sinus infections, allergies, and asthma reactions—all of which can make you quite ill.

Check for mold on the backside of bathroom throw rugs, in tile grout, and on walls and the ceiling. If you sneeze or wheeze in the bathroom, you might have a mold issue. Mold, or fungus, can develop on your skin like it does in your toenails. It can invade your lungs and cause allergy problems. Take aggressive steps to eliminate and prevent this potential problem. Shorter, cooler showers help—read on.

Chlorine: If you are on a city or town water system, the real fear is what comes out of your showerhead. Municipal water is treated with chlorine, a key component of dioxin. Dioxin has been rated by the Environmental Protection Agency (EPA) as being 300,000 times more potent a carcinogen than DDT. However, this danger is eliminated if the water treatment plant substitutes chloramine for chlorine. Contact your city municipal water system to find out if they substitute.

Americans ingest a daily amount of dioxin that is 300–600 times greater than the EPA's so-called "safe" dose due to chlorine pollution. If an item is white, such as typing paper, clothing, towels, or sanitary napkins, they have been bleached and the dioxin from the bleach will soak into your skin and build up in your body.

Dioxin mimics a steroidlike hormone, so it fools the body's standard chemical response into setting off a variety of physical effects. These effects include suppressed immunity, damage to major organs such as the liver, reproductive and developmental impairment, infertility, birth defects, and cancer.

What does chlorine in the water have to do with your shower? Heat expands a surface. Take metal, for instance. When you need to change the oil in your car and the filter is stuck, use a hair dryer. When heated, the chamber expands and the filter pops right out. When you shower, the hot water expands your pores, which allows for higher absorption of the organochlorines and trihalmethanes.

Dirty Words

According to The United Nations Environment Program, "Organochlorines are compounds that contain carbon, *chlorine*, and hydrogen. Their chlorine-carbon bonds are very strong. They are highly insoluble in water, but are attracted to fats." So they bioaccumulate in the body.

Dirty Words

When paper is bleached using chlorine, I-Dioxin is but one of the by-products of that manufacturing process. I-Dioxin is believed to be the single most carcinogenic chemical known to scientists. Use unbleached paper.

These two chlorine by-products have been linked to endometriosis, immune system impairment, diabetes, neurotoxicity, birth defects, decreased fertility, cancer, liver and organ disease, breathing problems, headaches, nosebleeds, and reproductive dysfunction in both women and men to name a few.

Now you can take that breath of fresh air. There is a solution for chlorinated water for both your drinking water and for your shower. Solve the problem by installing water filters, but do your research first. This website compares water filters for the kitchen and shower: www. waterfiltercomparisons.com. Also check *Consumer Guide*.

Tackle the Toilet

It seems to me that all these warnings about germs everywhere can be a bit heavy. When I was little, my grandparents had an outhouse on the farm. There wasn't a hand sanitizer available, yet plenty of not-so-nice stuff got splattered on the wooden rim.

We washed several times a day, especially before touching food. No one thought a thing about germs. In fact, studies by Professor Charles Gerba of the University of Arizona proved that the toilet seat is the least contaminated area in the home.

An excellent diet, plenty of exercise, and diligence to proper hygiene conquers the germs that sneak up on you in the bathroom. Use warm, soapy water and lather up for as long as it takes to sing "Happy Birthday." Skip the musical melody out in public—unless you have a good voice or your kids are with you. You can get by with being goofy in public as long as the kids are there.

Why sing Happy Birthday? Remember my number one rule to cleaning "Give your product time to work." It takes time for the soap to kill germs. Singing Happy Birthday is a fun way to remember to give the soap time to kill the germs.

Keep It Tidy

Talk about germ haven. All the "stuff" scattered on the bathroom counters, towels flung everywhere, yesterday's dirty cloths hanging from the doorknob. Nothing thoroughly dries so mold creeps up on you faster than the December holidays. Stash your toiletries on a shelf in hanging baskets or vanity drawers. Use a shower caddy that hangs from the showerhead to hold your shampoo bottles. Rev your engines and let's get into warp speed cleaning the bathroom.

Bad Ring Day

Whew, the toilet germs aren't so bad after all. "Least contaminated" is still contaminated, though, so let's learn a few tricks to beat back the dirt and germs.

Sprinkle baking soda around the inside of the toilet bowl. Pour in $\frac{1}{3}$ cup of white vinegar, and scrub with a nylon toilet bowl brush. Arm and Hammer baking soda now comes in a plastic container with holes on the top, which is perfect for cleaning jobs. Refill the bottle from the extra large boxes of baking soda and save the environment from another tossed plastic container.

Spray down the outside of the toilet weekly with the 50/50 vinegar and water solution, and wipe dry. If you have young kids who sometimes can't manage to hit the mark, you can use this mixture to disinfect, so keep a bottle handy in the bathroom.

Mary's Handy Hints

Use Nature's Miracle on flooring around the toilet where "accidents" happen. The enzymes kill the odor and germs.

Ring around the toilet! Don't let your toilet be mocked like the people in the old Whisk commercial. Back the water out of the bowl by putting on a rubber glove and plunging your hand down the opening a couple of times. Grab a product called Erase It for Bathrooms. Customers who use this product have reported to us that it has removed rings nothing else could budge.

Dirty Words

When my son was learning to "go like the big boys," he often missed the toilet. He loved games, so I invented the "shoot it down" game by placing a piece of toilet paper in the bowl for him to "shoot" down. He never missed after that!

Work your way around the ring with the Erase It. Alternatively, you can use a pumice stone. Be very, very careful using this stone, though, because it will scratch your bowl. Dampen the stone with water and gently (gently!) work a small area until some of the stone appears on the toilet. Switch to a janitorial toothbrush or a white scrubbie pad and finish cleaning the bowl.

Prevention Rules

After removing the ring and cleaning the toilet, spray a product called Advantage or your polymer-based car wax (yes, car wax) that does not contain petroleum distillates on the inside of the rinsed and dried bowl. Wipe to apply evenly. Let it dry for 10 minutes; then flush to return the water to the bowl. Polymer-based car waxes make a surface slick. We'll leave it to your imagination as to the benefits of a slick toilet bowl!

For even more prevention, once a month pour a cup of white vinegar into your toilet bowl and leave it overnight. The mild acid in the vinegar neutralizes the alkali in the water, preventing rings from forming. How often you treat your toilets depends on the hardness of your water. If monthly treatment isn't working, then step it up to twice a month.

When you leave to go out of town for an extended period, pour a cup of (guess what?) white vinegar in the toilet. Cover the bowl with plastic wrap. Plastic wrap helps to prevent the water from evaporating, which prevents water ring marks. That way, you can spend the month in Paris without worrying about your toilet! Please put a sticky note on the toilet as a reminder to remove the plastic wrap.

Once every three months, pour a couple cups of 3 percent hydrogen peroxide in the toilet tank. This prevents mold and mildew growth. Let it sit overnight, scrub, and flush.

Rust Be Gone

If rust is coming down through the little holes in the toilet bowl, you need to clean the inside of the tank. Shut off the valve and flush it to drain the tank. Dilute a concentrated cleaner like CleanEz or Bi-O-Kleen one part cleaner to four parts water. Spray the solution on the sides of the tank, and then scrub with Bon Ami or Barkeeper's Friend using a stiff bristled brush.

Remove those rust stains inside the toilet with the Erase It for Bathrooms. Those stains pop right out.

Counterattack

Now that you have put up a wall cabinet over the toilet and the clutter is cleared off the counter … um, the clutter is gone right? No? Okay, it's time to pull those drawers out and toss anything that hasn't been used in the last two years.

Use drawer dividers to separate your things. My drawers are narrow and the dividers are too wide. A 6 ounce cup holds things like nail clippers, tweezers, and any taller but round or narrow items that tend to get lost on the bottom of the drawer.

A small wire shelf (found at the hardware store) fits in the back of the main cabinet to stash bottles that aren't used often. I have more than two or three such bottles cluttering up my cabinets. They will get used—one of these days.

Scrubbing the Sink

Believe it or not, the place in the bathroom that harbors the most germs isn't the toilet—it's the sink drain! Once a month pour $\frac{1}{2}$ cup of baking soda down the drain and top it off with white vinegar. The resulting fizzing action will scour out the drain and eat its way through any soap scum or other gunk. If you are on a septic system, use the Nature's Miracle because baking soda will damage your tanks.

On a weekly basis, clean the sink with diluted all-purpose cleaner such as Bi-O-Kleen, CleanEz, or Red Juice by The Clean Team. A thin wire brush used for cleaning battery cables scrubs the drain hole at the top of the basin so it doesn't clog up. Who me? Forget to turn off the water causing the sink to overflow because I neglected this little detail? Never!

To clean soap scum from the sink, wipe it out with the all-purpose cleaner, undiluted. To get rid of that hard water ring around the drain, plug the drain and pour $\frac{1}{2}$ cup of white vinegar into the sink. Let it sit an hour; then scrub with a toothbrush and a bit of baking soda.

One Step Ahead in the Shower

My warnings about spraying cleaners in the air could not be more important than in the shower. The particles drift directly onto your face and right into your lungs. Even if you are using an ecosafe cleaner, it is foreign matter to your lungs and will irritate them. Most bathrooms are small, confined areas. Few have windows that can be opened. The smaller the space, the more the impact sprays have on your health.

Spray your cloth and then wipe mirrors and showers or tub enclosures. Your body is not made to process cleaners so keep them out of your face.

If you were to interview a bacterium and ask for its ideal vacation spot, you'd find that it's not too picky. "Oh, anyplace works—the warmer and damper, the better." Warm and damp like a bathroom? Yes, like a bathroom.

Mary's Handy Hints

We lived in Houston, Texas, where it was so humid you were drenched before you even had time to dry off after a shower. A dehumidifier finally won the battle of the mold.

Prevent bacteria from multiplying by ventilating the bathroom. Got a window? Crack it open as you begin to shower to remove the humidity and off-gassing from chlorinated water. No window? Turn on the fan and install a filter for the showerhead that removes the chlorine to prevent dioxin buildup. Wipe down the shower once a month with straight white vinegar to prevent and kill mold.

If you like to sing in the shower, you might hit a sour note if your shower walls and glass doors are covered with water spots and soap scum. Get back in tune by following these tips.

Fiberglass and Glass Doors

Alkalinity in the water causes those not-so-pretty spots on your glass doors and shower walls. To spite the spots, twice yearly apply the same polymer-based car wax you use in the toilet on shower walls and doors. Both fiberglass and glass are porous. Polymer car wax puts a slick barrier on any surface, including shower walls. Water sheets down rather than "sticking" on the walls to form unsightly and difficult-to-remove water marks.

Two tips on waxing the shower: first, make sure the wax does not contain petroleum distillates, which is harmful to your health. Never use distillates inside your home. Advantage, found at www. goclean.com, is distillate free and a good choice. Second, avoid spraying Advantage on shower walls because it drifts onto the floor—unless you're a fan of extreme showering. It makes the floor slick. Pour a bit on your cloth and then wipe it on.

Mary's Handy Hints

If you're tired of fighting the battle of the soap scum, switch to organic or glycerin soap. Lye and animal fat in bar soaps cause the buildup. Guess where else that soap scum builds up? Yep, in your drains. By changing soap, you get rid of the scum, clogged drains, and itchy skin.

Squeegee or wipe down your shower after each use. Combined with the car wax and switching soap, you'll clean the shower faster than you can sing your favorite melody. Clean the showers weekly using an organic concentrated cleaner. Dilute the cleaner according to bottle directions then pour it on a towel and wipe down the surface. Wait a few minutes and wipe it off.

Okay, so the soap scum refuses to budge and the Queen of England is coming for a visit. Bring out both barrels: use your organic concentrated cleaner full strength. Pour plenty on an damp dishrag and then wipe it on the walls and doors.

Patience now becomes a virtue. Wait and wait some more. Go clean the rest of the bedroom section of your home. Wipe the cleaner back on the walls when it starts to drip down the walls. Every so often, check the walls with a fingernail. If the residue removes easily, round one is almost over.

Dirty Words

Daily shower sprays keep your shower clean. However, inside your body the chemicals attach to fat cells, accumulating and build layer after layer of toxic residue on your liver, lungs, and other vital organs. They are costly to buy and to your health. Pass them by in the stores.

Use a white pad such as a Scotch-Brite pad to scrub. (Use the white ones only. The colored scrubbers are courser and do scratch.) Test a spot to make sure it won't scratch the fiberglass. Dampen the pad and gently scrub. This removes the soap buildup and most of the white mineral deposits on the glass doors. Nothing removes the etch marks themselves, but further damage is halted. Reapply the cleaner if necessary.

Tubs and Floors

You don't need chemical-laden tub sprays to clean your tub. After all, who wants to take a chemical bath? Try this instead:

1. Mix 3 tablespoons of a mild liquid dish detergent, a tablespoon or 2 of borax, and $1/2$ cup of vinegar. Then add 2 quarts of water and pour it into a spray bottle. Shake.

2. Thoroughly saturate a terry towel, wiping it on the side walls of the tub first. Begin at the bottom of the wall and work your way to the top.

3. Wait a minute, dampen a cloth, sprinkle it with a bit of baking soda, scrub, rinse, and then dry. Repeat with the tub.

Now light a candle, pour a cup of tea, and take a nice, hot bath—but only after you install a filter that removes the chlorine.

Ceramic Tile

The big debate: some experts claim that acids (such as our beloved white vinegar) will etch ceramic tile and corrode it. Others believe that a half-and-half solution of vinegar is much too mild to harm today's hardy ceramic finishes. We suggest using it only occasionally just to be safe.

Here's an easy homemade ceramic tile cleaner that will get your tiles all sparkly without acid or harmful chemicals:

1. Mix $\frac{1}{8}$ cup of mild laundry detergent with 2 quarts of water and pour it into a spray bottle.

2. Shake (the bottle, not yourself).

3. Saturate an old dish cloth and wipe the tiles.

4. Use a heavyweight terry towel to wipe the solution (and dirt) from the tub and walls. If needed, scrub with a white scrub pad dampened with the cleaning solution.

5. Wipe dry with a terry towel.

It's easy, cheap, and nontoxic. Why use foaming cleansers that cause health issues?

Grout Busters

When it's time to get tough, the tough get going but often are stopped dead in their tracks when it comes to removing mold from tile grout. People spray toxins like bleach on the grout trying to kill the mold. Their knuckles bleed from using scrubbing pads, and they have to call a masseuse to rub their tired arms. That is a lot of work to ruin your health with toxic sprays.

To clean dirty grout, try a product called The StainEraser, which is a flat bar created specifically for removing mold, mildew, dirt, and stains from grout—and it doesn't matter where the grout is located. On your floor, in your shower, or in the swimming pool, this little gadget works.

The open pores of grout are way too inviting for mold, soap scum (a good reason to switch soap), and stains. When they hit, they leave an ugly mess for you to clean. If The StainEraser doesn't work, mix a paste using borax and plaster the grout. Let it sit for 10 minutes; then tackle it with a firm toothbrush.

Next, spray the grout with a solution of half water and half 35 percent food-based hydrogen peroxide, which you can get at some health food stores. Wait from 30 to 45 minutes, and then spray it again. Let this sit on the grout all day to kill the mold and mildew.

> **Dirty Words**
>
> Prevention is key to eliminating mold. Take shorter, cooler showers. Turn on the fan and open the window. Steam also dries and warps cabinet doors and wrecks paint. If your shower curtain is long enough, cut off the seam at the bottom to prevent mildew buildup in the seam.

After you have won the battle of the mold, head to a store specializing in tile for a nontoxic bottle of a five-year grout sealer. You can use their sponge applicators, but the easier way to apply grout is to head to a Western Supply store. Ask for the syringes used to give horses and cattle shots. Buy a couple in case you need extra. They come in handy for a lot of cleaning jobs.

Carefully remove the needle. Suck up the sealer into the syringe and go. The syringe allows you to apply the sealer without spilling it all over the tile. After the first application, wait five days and then apply a second coat. Congratulations! You have won the war against grout mongers.

It's Curtain Time

Plastic shower curtains are certainly much less expensive than other kinds of curtains. They are waterproof so the floor doesn't take a shower along with you.

However, there is a dark side to vinyl. Chapter 2 discloses the dangers of vinyl flooring. Vinyl shower curtains contain the same polyvinyl chloride (PVC) as vinyl flooring, and this PVC releases volatile organic chemicals (VOCs) into the air, which increases respiratory problems and cancer. Should vinyl catch on fire, it's deadly.

Add vinyl flooring to the vinyl curtains and you have a double whammy of toxic gasses pouring into your bathroom. That does not include the adhesive used to lay the flooring or the adhesive in the cabinets. Bathrooms are smaller areas so the impact of these poisenous gasses multiplies due to the concentration.

There are alternative and much safer curtains. Look for ones made with nylon, Tyvek, cotton, linen, or hemp. Nylon and Tyvek are not natural materials but are safe to use. Cotton and linen are natural alternatives, with cotton being easier to launder. Although quite expensive, hemp does not mold or mildew—now there is a breath of fresh air. It is machine washable and lasts for decades.

Spray curtains with your all-purpose cleaner. Wait 10 minutes and wash with your rags, which provide a scrubbing action. Air dry.

Faucets and Showerheads

Most faucets and showerheads are made from chrome or brushed nickel. Clean them with your all-purpose cleaner. Remove water spots with straight vinegar. Rust spots disappear with a bit of elbow grease, fresh lemon juice, and salt.

Brass, plated brass, and gold-plated faucets must be dried after each use. They are beautiful, but they do discolor. The discoloration is difficult to remove. Jeweler's rouge (found at jewelry lapidary supply stores or better jewelry stores) is best for cleaning them. Always follow the manufacturer's directions.

Occasionally, remove your showerheads and soak them overnight in white vinegar to remove the buildup and dirt that clogs the holes. If you can't remove the showerhead, fasten a zipper plastic bag full of vinegar around the showerhead using string or boxing tape. Do not use duct tape because it won't hold.

Dirty Words

Do not use rubber-backed mats on any kind of flooring. They leave yellow stains on the floor that you can never remove. Use a light-colored cotton rug and nonslip pads, which don't stain the floor.

Monsters in Your Drains

Down in the deep dark dredges lays this murky mess. Little wonder it erupts like a geyser, considering its daily feeding regime.

Consider this: the soap you use in your shower and sink is made with lye and animal fat. It creates soap scum on shower walls *and* in the drains. Hair washes down the drain, sticking to the soap scum. The drain begins to clog so the water can't drain properly. It then turns to green slimy mold. All of a sudden that poor drain rebels and coughs this mess back up to you.

So you grab a jar of toxic drain opener, adding to the toxic waste headed to the municipal water treatment plant. Yes, that is the same water with which you shower, drink, and cook.

Just like your kitchen drains, pour a cup of Nature's Miracle down those drains once a month before retiring to prevent the clogs. Clear clogged drains with $1/2$ cup of baking soda followed by a cup of vinegar. Repeat nightly if needed. Borax can be used in conjunction with baking soda: $1/4$ cup of each.

Reflections on You: Mirrors

Most people don't spring out of bed ready to tackle whatever the day may bring. One glance in the bathroom mirror and those tall tale crows feet tattle on you. You don't need a streaky mirror emphasizing the crow's feet.

Nor does your body need the toxic chemicals found in most store-bought window cleaners. Think crow's feet on your liver, kidneys, lungs, and respiratory tract. The diethylene glycol and ammonia found in these cleaners can turn healthy organ cells into scar tissue resembling crow's feet. Refer to Chapter 4 for healthy and cheaper alternative glass cleaners.

Lowdown on Floors

We're almost done and the battle-weary bacteria are looking for rein-forcements. They have no place left to hide except the place that's easi-est to overlook: the floor.

Don't think you can just stomp up and down on the little critters; they're a bit hardier than that. No, you need to marshal your forces for one final assault. Check out Chapter 10 for the scoop on cleaning floors.

The Least You Need to Know

- ◆ Proper hygiene is as important as cleaning when it comes to pro-tecting yourself and your family from illness.

- ◆ Dampness is a bathroom's worst enemy because it causes mold and mildew, warped cabinets, and allergy-irritating smells—so venti-late!

- ◆ Never use bleach or other toxic chemicals, and always wipe the cleaner on the surface rather than spraying.

- ◆ Wipe down the shower after each use; then seal grout to prevent mold, mildew, and buildup.

Chapter 8

Beautiful Bedrooms

In This Chapter

- ◆ Maintaining your mattress
- ◆ Are your sheets making you sick?
- ◆ Making a case for pillow cleanliness
- ◆ Clearing the closet

When my son, Jason, was 3 years old, he crept into my bedroom one morning around 3 A.M. Without a doubt, he thought long and hard for something to say so he would not be returned to his own bed. Jason put his arm over my shoulder and said, "It's be ok Mommy, I's love you."

To this day, I cannot enter a bedroom without hearing those precious words. Only there are some not-so-precious things happening in the bedroom. Dust mites, mold, as well as fumes from mattresses and pillows, all contribute to health issues.

Well, your home is not "green" until you put the boot to the backsides of these problems. You spend eight hours a day in your bedroom, so let's green clean it and keep it toxin free.

Clearing Clutter

I cleaned homes professionally and heard so many excuses as to why the clutter built up that I could write an *Idiot's Guide* on clutter excuses. Dust mites, mold, and mildew cling to moisture. Air cannot circulate around clutter to dry it out; therefore, moisture develops and so do dust mites and mold.

What damage can a few dust mites cause? Dust mites invade a home by the millions, and they love moisture, especially around areas that lack breathability such as clutter, mattresses, foam pillows, and tight spaces under the bed or behind dressers.

The fecal matter left by dust mites causes allergic reactions. Yes, you are laying your body and your head on top of fecal matter every night and then waking up to a stuffy nose and worse.

First things first—clear the clutter. You can't clean a room when tripping over books, dusting around toys, and vacuuming up socks. Reread Chapter 1 and ransack your bedroom.

Here are a few ideas to help you tidy up:

◆ Cardboard stacking boxes with pull out drawers make quick hideaways for smaller items. Avoid plastic because it off-gasses toxic fumes. Those fumes take years to dissipate.

◆ Purchase a hanger at a department store that hooks over your door for a quick way to hang up your robe or often-used sweatshirts or pants.

◆ Do not store items under your bed because the tighter quarters are an open invitation for mold and dust mites. Rather, look into a bed with built-in drawers. The solid base eliminates the need to buy box springs and saves our Earth and your budget.

◆ Wood closet organizers keep things stowed neatly away. Paint them with a sealer to prevent the off-gassing of the adhesive in particle board. Better yet, explore second-hand stores for shelving or book cases. This furniture has off-gassed, and it's recycled and can be painted. What a winning combo!

Mattress Matters

Here I go getting serious again, but the toxic fumes in furniture, carpet, floor, your mattress, and pillows are no laughing matter. Most foam mattresses are made of polyurethane, which off-gasses volatile organic chemicals (VOCs) and can cause many health issues.

Because mattresses are made from flammable material, it is required that they be treated with PBDE (see "Lurking in Your Furniture" in Chapter 2 for a discussion of PBDE). Foam releases toluene diisocyanate, which can cause severe lung problems. Stain-resistant chemicals added to mattresses are also toxic. Anything that does not breathe, like dense foam, is a welcome mat to dust mites and mold.

Switch to latex mattresses, and look for ones that are green with no toxic chemicals; check out www.latexmattresscompany.com; or you can cover your mattress and pillows see www.achooallergy.com. They carry chemical free sheets, bedding, mattress, pillow covers, and dust mite covers.

I can't solve the problem of your partner hogging the bed or the sheets, but the following will keep your mattress in good shape:

 Mary's Handy Hints

Ripping off mattress tags won't hurt a thing until you discover the mattress is defective. If that tag is gone, so is your warranty. Leave tags on mattresses, sofas, and chairs.

- ◆ Wash the mattress protective cover at least once a month. Vacuum the mattress monthly as well to remove dust mites.

- ◆ Turn your mattress every two weeks to keep the padding evenly distributed. You'll sleep better and extend the life of the mattress. One week flip the mattress over; the next turn it from end to end. Consult the manufacturer before flipping newer mattresses.

- ◆ Make sure your frame has a middle bar support so the mattress won't bow in the middle.

- ◆ When you need to replace your mattress, look for one that is not chemically treated and not made from foam. Stay away from foam memory pad toppers. Stick to cotton, bamboo, or latex, unless you are allergic to latex.

Follow these tips and you'll be sleeping soundly.

Pillow Talk

I don't recommend reading this chapter at night before you go to sleep. It could give you nightmares knowing you are about to lay your head on the fecal matter left by dust mites.

Pillow cases contain dyes, pesticides, flame retardants, fertilizers (you read correctly), and wrinkle-resistant chemicals that greet you every night. They harm our lakes, our streams, our soil, and your family's health and can cause memory loss.

Polyester sheets and pillow cases are made from softened thermoplastic, a petrochemical, although the "no-iron" sheets and cotton/blend wrinkle-resistant sheets are the worst offenders. They are treated with a formaldehyde resin.

Make sure your sheets don't say "easy care" or "no-iron." Turn to "green sheets" made from unbleached cotton, bamboo, or hemp. Search the internet to compare prices and selections. A good place to start is www.Ecomall.com.

Sneeze or Snooze

You wake up every morning exhausted, achy, and sneezing. You won't find the culprit under your nose—but under your head.

A common cause of allergy woes is what's living in your pillow: dust mites. Dust mites are microscopic arachnids that feed on shed human skin. As we inhale them, our membranes respond and we get congested. Switch to a cotton or latex pillow and then cover it with a dust mite protective cover. A dehumidifier also helps.

Not only do you breathe dust mite fecal matter all night, but your nose is also directly on top of a chemical-laden pillow. These are the same toxins that off-gas from curtains, carpet, and furniture. They include toluene diisocyanate and formaldehyde, which can cause allergic reactions and cancer.

Keeping Your Pillow Pure

After you've discovered the best pillow, it's simply a matter of taking good care of it so it keeps its shape and isn't an open door to dust mites. Follow these tips for a clean pillow:

◆ **Buckwheat hull pillows.** When purchasing buckwheat pillows, make sure they're "99 percent clean." The hulls can contain excess dust, which causes sinus problems. Never wash or dampen buckwheat hulls. Wash only the zippered case. Freeze the pillows to kill mites or other crawly creatures that might drop in for a visit. Add more buckwheat as needed when it "polishes" down with use.

Dirty Words

Never put a damp pillow into a pillow case. It will mold and mildew, ending up as another discarded item in a landfill.

◆ **Down pillows.** Most often the feathers for down pillows are removed from living or just-slaughtered fowl. They are then bleached, sterilized, and treated with chemicals. Chemicals are then added to the feathers to hold them together.

Although you can machine wash down pillows, they will last longer if you hand wash them. Do so by submerging them in the tub using Brown Sheep Shampoo, found in yarn shops or online. Squeeze out all the air and submerge them in the water for two hours. Rinse with a tub full of water plus $\frac{1}{2}$ cup of white vinegar. Dry the pillows in the dryer on a low setting, removing them frequently to refluff.

◆ **Foam pillows.** Hand-wash foam pillows in the tub using an organic soap. Press on the pillow to work the soap into the pillow and let it soak for 30 minutes. Rinse by adding $\frac{1}{2}$ cup of white vinegar to the rinse water. Again, press the water into the pillow to remove the soap. Air dry only because foam will catch on fire in the dryer, even on the air dry setting.

◆ **Polyester pillows.** They can be washed in a front-loading washer; otherwise, take these pillows to a laundromat and wash them in a large-capacity washer. They are bulky and can damage a top-loading washer. Use an organic detergent that does not contain a whitening agent or bleach. Use $\frac{1}{4}$ cup of white vinegar in the rinse to remove detergent residue. Machine dry on low heat.

◆ **Wool pillows.** Follow the cleaning directions that come with the pillow. Moths can invade wool pillows so stick to chemical-free cotton or latex pillows (unless you have latex allergies) for a good night's sleep. Pillow protectors that go under pillow cases prevent hair oil from damaging the pillow.

Making the Bed

Sheets and pillow cases do more than keep you comfy—they protect your bedding and keep it clean. The bottom sheet protects your mattress. The top sheet keeps you warm and protects the blanket from skin oils and dirt.

You don't *have* to make the bed, but not doing so means that at night, when all you want is a comfortable bed, you'll find one that is crumpled rather than an inviting haven. Besides, air cannot circulate around crumpled bedding, which opens the door to mold and mites.

Speaking of Sheets

Launder your bedding weekly to remove dust, body oil, and the mites that have taken up residence in the sheets. Also, frequent laundering helps to break down the chemicals that have been added to sheets. Never put new sheets on a bed without laundering them at least twice.

To help reduce dust mites, throw back the covers and air out your bed every morning while you shower. We lose body fluid during the night, especially when we are ill or during menopause. The dampness encourages mold and dust mite populations.

Blankets and More

As you snuggle up at night under your blankets, make sure they are as free of VOCs as your pillows and sheets. Use 100 percent unbleached cotton, hemp, or bamboo; then enjoy a sound night's sleep. Clean blankets at least every 3 or 4 months, following the manufacturer's instructions.

Now that you have a fresh start on your bedding and pillows, let's quickly make your bed:

- ◆ After you put on your fitted sheet, place the flat sheet on top with the larger hem at the head of the bed.

- ◆ Miter your blanket corner the same as you did for the flat sheet. Fold the top of the top sheet over the blanket to protect the blanket as you sleep.

- ◆ Toss the comforter or duvet on the bed (leaving it untucked).

- ◆ Finally, arrange your pillows in any way that makes you happy.

Mary's Handy Hints _____

For mitered corners, tuck in the bottom edge of the sheet. Pick up the corner of the sheet and bring it around to the side of the bed. Put the side of the sheet up out of your way on the bed. Tuck in the part of the sheet that's left hanging down, and then let the corner fall and tuck in the side of the sheet near the foot of the bed. Done! A bed any army sergeant would be proud of. (Can you bounce a quarter off of it? Even better!)

When you make your bed in the morning, simply pull the covers up over your pillows. It takes less than 30 seconds when your bed is properly made after changing the sheets.

Cleaning the Closet

It's easy to get yourself in and out of tight spots. Getting the clutter out of tight spots inside a closet gets you into better health. You have read that tight spots promote moisture, mold, and dust mites. Did you realize that mold and dust mites migrate to your clothing? That happens easily in closets where clutter is in close proximity to clothing.

Keeping things tucked onto shelves or inside storage boxes reduces floor clutter. It's easier to vacuum a floor when you have two or three boxes to pull out rather than six or seven piles of stuff. Spritz the floor lightly with an essential oil that kills bugs like clove or geranium; then vacuum.

Reduce mite and mold infestation in closets by switching from carpet to a painted cement floor or linoleum—never vinyl. Cedar wood floors help fight bug infestations in closets.

Clean the Unseen

Talk about wanting to close the door because if you don't see the dirt you don't have to clean it. That pretty much sums up most people's opinion about cleaning closets. We are so hesitant to part with our possessions that the back of our closets double for the Goodwill store. So, we shut the door and hope nothing tumbles down when we open it again.

Keep the Closet Clean

If it has been over five years since your last good closet cleaning, put down this book and go tackle this job. We promise we'll be here waiting when you finish.

Follow these steps for a refreshingly new closet:

1. Clear all your clothes out of the closet and put them on the bed. All other items go into boxes.

   Remember: If you haven't worn it in the past three years, it's good-bye time. And, yes, it's fine to toss the gaudy shirt you were given for last year's birthday.

2. Sort your belongings into three piles: To Keep, To Give Away, and To Toss. Shake the dust out of any clothes you are going to keep before hanging them back up—but shake them outside!

3. Vacuum the closet and wipe down the walls and shelves with a damp cloth.

4. Banish mold and mildew. If the closet smells musty, find the source of the mold and treat it. Refer to Chapter 4 for recipes.

5. Clean the floors according to the instructions in Chapter 10.

6. Put the clothing back and arrange it either per the season or how often you wear it. For example, keep all slacks in one area and shirts in another. More frequently worn clothing should be hung where they are easily accessible.

Mary's Handy Hints

Store shoes on a shoe rack. Some experts recommend stowing them away in boxes, but they need to air dry to prevent mold.

Is your closet clean yet? Think of how much time you'll save when you don't spend 10 minutes looking for one pair of slacks. Then say your farewells to at least a million dust mites.

The Least You Need to Know

◆ Clearing the clutter makes cleaning easier.

◆ Get creative with storage ideas to keep things tucked away.

◆ You'll sleep better on a cotton or latex pillow that does not contain petroleum products or formaldehyde.

◆ Walk into a refreshing and restful bedroom by keeping it picked up and the bed made.

◆ Research before buying bedding, pillows, and mattresses to eliminate off-gassing from added chemicals: check out the resource section for suggestions.

Chapter 9

Lovely Living Rooms

In This Chapter

◆ The who, what, when, and care of hard wood furniture

◆ When upholstered furniture needs attention

◆ Caring for window coverings

◆ All about knickknacks, lampshades, paintings, and more

The living room could also be called the "not-so-living room" depending on its stage of disarray. After the dinner dishes are cleared and cleaned, family members gather in this room to read, play a game, put puzzles together, or catch up on *American Idol*.

Keeping the living room clean can be tricky with so many projects going on at one time. All goes well until unexpected company pounds on the front door and, of course, expects to hang out in the living room, projects and all. A trip through this chapter provides the clues to clean up, declutter, and find a peaceful balance.

Decluttering the Living Room

Reading about all the health issues connected with mold and dust mites should have been enough to get you hustling the clutter out of your home. But how do you organize project "clutter" in a room that is used in so many ways—so often?

You read in organizational articles to make piles when sorting things. Piles such as Discard, Keep, Goodwill, and Garage Sale. Begin your descent on living room clutter with the largest pile. As you sort, put items being currently used in the Keep pile until it has worn out its welcome.

Next, organize the Keep pile so you stay in control of the clutter. A magazine rack keeps magazines neat and tidy. Search a second-hand store for an older chest. They make attractive catch alls for games, puzzles, and knitting projects. Older furniture has gassed off toxic fumes from paints and adhesives, plus no tree needs sacrificing to make yet another chest. A stereo unit with doors hides frequently used books.

Polish: What's Hot, What's Not

Wax on, wax off might have been simple for Mr. Miyagi, but it's not that simple with wood furniture. First, you must determine whether your furniture has a hard finish or an oil finish.

A hard finish is shiny like a polyurethane wood floor and feels slick to the touch. Oil finishes have a natural look. Run your hand over them, and you can feel the grain.

Always dust and polish wood furniture with the grain of the wood to prevent scratches.

 Dirty Words

Stay away from polishes containing silicone and petroleum distillates. Distillates are toxic and should never be used inside the home. Both distillates and silicone can soften the sealant on finishes. Call the manufacturer or look online for the material safety data sheet (MSDS) before using a wood care product.

Hard Finishes

Wood furniture with a hard finish needs a weekly wiping with a barely damp cloth. Dry it with a soft, clean cloth.

A product such as Guardsman can be used on hard finishes. You might have read that wax causes a build-up on furniture. We are here to debunk that myth. Natural beeswax does not build up. The culprits are the chemicals added to the wax. They soften the finish so it looks dull and cloudy and feels sticky.

Antiques

Use only a dry, soft, 100 percent cotton cloth like a baby diaper to dust antique furniture. Use a slightly damp cloth if the antique furniture has been restored. Never use a wood treatment on antique furniture that has the original black lacquered finish.

Oil, Satin-Gloss, and Low-Gloss Finishes

Treat oil, satin-gloss, and low-gloss finishes with cream waxes or liquid cleaning polishes that do not contain silicones or distillates; try The Clean Team polish. Always use a soft 100 percent cotton cloth, such as cloth diapers. Buff the wood and then dry it. How often you condition this wood depends on where you live. If you live in a dry or humid climate, treat the furniture three to four times per year. Twice a year is fine in other climates. Increase the frequency if you see signs of drying or warping.

Leather, Vinyl, Ultra Leather, and Ultra Suede

Refer to Chapter 1 for the dangers of vinyl furniture. If you can't afford real leather, turn to natural untreated fabric furniture. Here's how to keep your leather and vinyl clean and prevent drying and cracking:

- ◆ Never use saddle soap, strong detergents or soaps, oils, furniture polish, ammonia, abrasive chemicals, alcohol, or other harsh cleaners to clean leather, vinyl, or ultra leather.

♦ Immediately clean any spill with a barely damp cloth and luke-warm water. Dab on a bit of mild cleanser such as baby shampoo; then dry it immediately.

♦ Dust leather furniture weekly with a barely damp cloth.

♦ Deep clean and condition your leather, vinyl, and ultra leather at least twice a year to prevent drying and cracking.

Mary's Handy Hints

If you have young children or pets, buy a plastic tablecloth. Turn the tablecloth upside-down on furniture and then top it with a bath towel. The towel absorbs the urine while the plastic prevents it from soaking through to the furniture. Use them to protect bedding and under children's seats at the table.

You can find a good leather cleaner and conditioner in western supply stores. Use conditioners made for soft leather such as vests, not those made for hard leather like boots. Make certain the cleaner won't darken the material and that it contains no silicone, petroleum distillates, or other harsh solvents.

Upholstery Tips

Back in the olden days, Grandma had to guess how to clean upholstered furniture—that's why she covered her furniture.

Today's furniture carries a cleaning code, which is printed on a label under the seat cushion. Now if only you knew what the cryptic *S* or *X* stood for. Here is what the codes mean:

♦ **W**—Use cool water only. Fabrics have changed and using even a mild detergent can leave stains. Avoid overwetting the fabric.

♦ **S**—Use solvent cleaner. Solvent cleaners are highly toxic and flammable. They should never be used in the home. Try foaming shaving cream. Test a very small spot first. Spray on a bit, wait 5 minutes, and then blot to rinse.

♦ **S-W**—Use water-based or solvent cleaner. Use water only due to toxic levels of solvents. You can use foaming shaving cream.

◆ **X**—Vacuum only. Clean this fabric only by vacuuming or a "dry sponge" to prevent accumulation of dust and grime. Remember that accumulated dirt is a haven for dust mites.

The use of a water-based solvent cleaner can cause spotting or excessive shrinking. Test an inconspicuous spot first. The toxins in these cleaners bioaccumulate in your body and are carcinogenic.

Mary's Handy Hints

When cleaning upholstery with detergent, rinse the area with ½ cup of white vinegar per gallon of water. Vinegar removes the soap residue to prevent dirt from clinging to the cleanser left in the fabric. It will stay cleaner far longer.

Curtains, Shades, and Blinds

After reading the dangers lurking behind window coverings, here is how you clean them. Window coverings keep sunlight from fading furnishings. They keep your home warm in the winter and cool in the summer, and keep stares from neighbors outside.

Vacuum your curtains monthly with the upholstery nozzle and the vacuum set at low suction. Use short strokes moving from top to bottom. Always clean the nozzle first in sudsy water (air dry thoroughly) so dirt won't transfer to the curtain.

Think twice before having your curtains dry cleaned. The chemicals used by dry cleaners can cause cancer and a host of other ailments. If they can be laundered, wash them on the gentle cycle and cool water. Hang them on a clothesline to dry.

Drapes deteriorate quickly exposed to the sun so they might not tolerate washing. They can be put in the dryer on air to bring out the dust. Or hang them on the clothesline on a windy day.

Mini Blind Beware

To clean them, turn the slats downward facing you. Spray a soft cloth with an all-purpose cleaner. (An old but clean cotton tube sock placed over one hand makes this job zip by in seconds.) Start at the top and wipe over the surface. Reverse the slats, pull the blinds out, and walk behind them. Repeat from the back. Do one room every time you dust to keep ahead of the buildup.

If mini blinds have reached the point of no return, grab a hammer and two good-size nails. Measure the blinds. Hammer the nails into the back of your home 1 foot less than the width of the blinds. Hang the blinds from the nails and turn the slats downward. With your all-purpose cleaner, begin spraying your way from the bottom to the top. Wipe them with a wet sponge when the cleaner drips from the top. Reverse the slats, flip the blinds over, and repeat from the back. Dry.

If you can't hang them outside, lay down nonslip pads in the bathtub to cover the floor of the tub. Fill the tub with warm (not hot) water and a bit of hair shampoo. Clean the slats one by one with a sponge. Rinse and dry them on a large beach towel.

To clean dingy cords, take a blob of foaming (non-gel) shaving cream and rub it onto the cords. Wait 30 minutes and then rinse with a solution of $\frac{1}{4}$ cup vinegar to 1 quart of water.

Wooden Blinds

Use only a solution of $\frac{1}{4}$ cup of white vinegar per quart of water to clean these blinds. Follow the directions for cleaning mini blinds with a cloth or sock. Do this once a month to prevent dirt from deteriorating the finish.

Fabric Pleated Shades

Never use water or cleaners on these shades unless you are fond of unsightly stains and damaged fabric. If you use a vacuum brush, clean the bristles frequently. Life should be easy, and the easy way to clean them is with a chemically treated dry sponge. (See Appendix B for information on where to buy these.) Use it dry and wipe over the shades. It's amazing how much dirt it removes!

Problems arise when bugs crawl across fabric blinds, leaving their ... um ... "bug spit" behind. Dampen a cotton swab with water, and then dip it in a bit of hair shampoo dabbing it on the stain. The swab prevents the shampoo from spreading on the shade. Let it set 10 minutes and gently blot it with a soft cloth like an old, clean, white cotton T-shirt.

Mary's Handy Hints

Use a dry sponge or a new 1 1/2 inch paintbrush to remove cobwebs and other nuisances from the tops of blinds and shades.

Vertical Shades

The dry sponge works best for vertical shades. You can roll them with a lint roller, although we have found that these shades don't collect dust like the horizontal shades.

The Small Stuff Counts, Too

The series of books *Don't Sweat the Small Stuff* remind us to let go of the small annoyances in life. However, your living room is filled with "small stuff" like lampshades and paintings. Don't let them get you sweating! Here's how to quickly clean them.

Mary's Handy Hints

If you insist on using a vacuum brush to clean lampshades, here's a solution. Cut off the leg of an old pair of pantyhose and slide it over the brush. Shift the panty hose leg as it soils.

Lampshades

Many experts advise cleaning cloth lampshades with the brush attachment of a vacuum cleaner. Didn't you just use it to remove dog hair from the La-Z-Boy? The dirt clinging to the brush will transfer to the shade, and the stiff bristles can damage shades.

A pastry or paint brush made of horsehair is the safest way to dust lampshades. Cut off the bristles 1/2 inch from the top at an angle to make them stiffer for easier cleaning. Finish with a "dry sponge."

If the lampshade can be washed, do so in the tub following the manufacturer's directions. Metal can rust (remember what happened to the poor Tin Man?), so dry shades with a hair dryer set to medium heat. Here are the directions:

1. Lay a rubber nonslip pad in the bottom of the tub and partially fill the tub with lukewarm water, adding a bit of baby shampoo.

2. Wash the shade with a soft cloth; then lightly rinse it.

3. Turn the shade upside down on a towel so the water runs out of the seams. Dry the metal parts with a hair dryer set to medium heat to prevent them from rusting.

Place glass lampshades and fixtures on a towel on the counter. Lightly spritz a soft cloth, like a clean old T-shirt, with organic window cleaner. Wipe and dry a section at a time.

Ceiling Fans

You can use your handy fan brush, which has an extension pole and bendable flat head to give the ceiling fan blades a good dusting. For a more thorough cleaning, pull a white cotton sock over the flat head and lightly spray the sock with a solution of ¼ cup white vinegar per quart of water.

> **Cleaning Quips**
>
> "God made rainy days so gardeners could get the housework done." Author unknown

Bend the duster and then run it across each blade. This method does a great job on the base of the fan as well, except use plain water, no vinegar, to keep from tarnishing any gold plating on the fan base.

Paintings

Pictures should never be hung in direct sunlight or near a window where dust gathers quickly and sun fades the paint on an oil painting. Kitchen steam and cooking oil damages them, as does cigarette and candle smoke.

Humidity also takes its toll on pictures, so a dehumidifier is a must-have for those in humid areas. Dust glass frequently with your dry dusting cloth. Lightly spray a bit of window cleaner on a cloth wiping over the glass to clean it. *Never* clean near the edge because liquid could seep under the glass. *Never* spray anything in the air near the painting. Liquids hang in the air and can damage the frame. Spray a cloth and then wipe.

Uncovered oil paintings need dusting once a year. Use a pastry brush made from horse hair or boar's hair. You'll find them at kitchen supply stores. Start at the top and gently brush your way to the bottom. Never use a vacuum cleaner brush or a duster because the dirt and oil on them will damage the painting.

Knickknacks

Have you put your knickknacks behind glass yet? No? Then they need a dusting two or three times a week with a real feather duster. Or you can wipe them with a soft flannel cloth. Heed my warnings about microfiber cloths and don't use them to dust.

For really dusty figurines, fill a rubber tub half full with warm water and add a squirt of baby shampoo. Put a towel on the bottom of the pan. Soak them for a minute and then clean them with the flannel cloth. Use a cotton swab or small foam paint brush to clean those small crevices.

Place small cloth items in a laundry bag with a barely damp cloth. Run them for 5–10 minutes in the dryer on the air setting—no heat. Or you can wipe them with a clean "dry sponge."

Chandeliers

Lamp stores and The Clean Team carry spray cleaners that remove dust buildup on chandelier teardrops without needing to remove them. Move all furniture aside and cover any other furniture and flooring with plastic. Place towels on top of the plastic to catch the drips.

Spray the teardrops and let them drip dry. As they are drying, wipe all the metal parts with a barely damp flannel cloth, drying as you go. Alternatively, you can remove the teardrops and place them in a rubber tub. Spray them with the cleaner.

For solid glass chandeliers, use a lambswool duster first to remove cobwebs. Wipe the metal with a barely damp flannel cloth. Place a piece of flannel cloth over the duster, rubber banding it around the handle. Lightly spritz the cloth with your window cleaner and go over both sides of the glass.

TVs

Always follow the manufacturer's guidelines when cleaning your TV. Unplug the set first, and then use a soft, barely damp cloth to clean the console. Never spray a cleaner directly on a TV. Liquids drip into the interior and damages the circuits and screen. Never touch the screen because oil from your hands can damage it.

When cleaning a TV screen, wipe with the grain of the screen; otherwise, you will scratch the surface. Other cleaning experts recommend using microfiber to clean a TV set. Never use a microfiber cloth on a TV screen. It will scratch the cabinet and the screen. Use a soft flannel material only.

Clean a CRT cathode-ray tube (CRT) TV by lightly spritzing your organic glass cleaner on a cloth. Carefully wipe.

Liquid crystal display (LCD), plasma screen TVs, and the newest liquid crystal on silicon (LCoS) televisions should never be cleaned with any cleaning product or even water. Gently dust them with a flannel cotton cloth. Keep all hands off deck on these TVs.

The Least You Need to Know

- Decluttering makes cleaning easier.
- Thanks to the magic of fabric codes, it's easy to know how to clean upholstered furniture.
- Know the finish of your wood before cleaning or conditioning it.
- With the right tools, you can keep your furnishings looking new without spending hours sweating over each item.

Part **3**

The Big Stuff

When it comes to cleaning, the big stuff counts, too. The best of cleaning professionals, including myself, can find a hundred little chores to keep us busy so we don't have to look at the big picture. And only the big stuff needs TLC! From floors to ceilings; windows to walls; gutters to cars—these areas need proper attention. In this part you'll learn how to shine your car, shape up your windows, and shake out the cobwebs. Plus you'll learn to do it without toxic cleaners.

Chapter 10

Hit the Floor Running

In This Chapter

- ◆ Rx for carpet
- ◆ Pining for clean wood floors
- ◆ Making vinyl vibrant
- ◆ All about stone, cork, and bamboo floors

Imagine how your floors must feel being walked on, trodden on, and underfoot all day. They take the brunt of what you drag in on your shoes from the great outdoors—things like oil from the street, dog deposits from the neighborhood park, and dirt and grit from your yard. When you come inside, all that gets mercilessly ground into your carpet and hard floor surfaces.

In an attempt to make amends and return the floor to its original pristine condition, you use the wrong cleaner and wear away the floor's protective coverings.

Tell your floor to fear no more. By the end of this chapter, you'll know how to keep it clean whether it's covered in carpet, topped with tiles, or housed with hardwood.

The Clean Sweep

After you meander across a grassy lawn, take a look down—at the bottom of your shoes, that is. You'll find sand, dirt, and pieces of grass. Walk across the carpet and all that dirt sticks to the buildup of oil already in your carpet. The dirt and oil become long-lost buddies who stick together no matter how hard your vacuum tries to extract them.

That dirt builds until you either rent a machine or call a professional carpet cleaner to clean the carpets. You rave over how nice the carpet looks, until two weeks later when it starts looking dirtier than it did before it was cleaned.

What confounded your cleaning efforts? Ever use a detergent to clean your vinyl floors and noticed that your feet stuck to the floor afterwards? The soap residue does not rinse clean and makes the floor sticky. The same thing happens with carpeting. The chemicals left in your carpet become a nesting ground for dirt. Like baby birds, the dirt won't fly the coop until it's forced to leave.

Mary's Handy Hints

Revisit Appendix A for a refresher course on how to blot and remove carpet stains. When you hire a carpet cleaning company, remember to get the material safety data sheets (MSDS) for the products they use and make sure the products are "green."

Even worse, the cleaning chemicals have probably exposed you to highly toxic fumes. The same solvents used at dry cleaners are often used on carpets. Don't forget the formaldehyde, lye, disinfectants, acids, and fragrances added to the cleaners. That toxic cocktail has been linked to many ailments.

By now, you might be fretting over the past ills you've inflicted on your carpet. Don't fret! Use the following solutions to keep your wall-to-wall on the ball.

Get a Grip on Vacuuming

Chapter 3 walked you through the basics of vacuum cleaners. Hopefully the slogan "Good ain't cheap and cheap ain't good" has engraved itself into your mind forever. Say you spend $4,000 to carpet your home. To cut costs, you purchase a $150 vacuum to clean it. Ten years later you spend $5,000 for new carpeting because dirt has been ground into the carpet and your $150 machine could not bring it out, thus wearing the carpet out. With proper care and a good vacuum, high-quality all-natural carpet should last 15–20 years.

We all love to breeze through cleaning as quickly as possible. Put on the breaks when you vacuum. It takes a bit of time for a vacuum's suction to inhale that deeply embedded dirt. Slow down and take your time, especially on the main traffic areas.

Kick the Habit

Basic carpet care 101: if dirt doesn't invade the carpet, the carpet stays cleaner. Because 80 percent of the dirt is drug in on your shoes, doesn't it make sense to kick them off at the door?

Oil from the bottom of your feet can damage carpet, so slip into a pair of clean socks. Some people with foot problems must wear shoes indoors, so keep your indoor shoes handy at the front door.

Dirt Beware

Even if you ditch the shoes at the door, carpet tends to be a dirt magnet. Counterattack it by vacuuming high-traffic areas daily if necessary followed with a thorough vacuuming once a week. When you set your cleaning schedule, consider things like pets, kids, and whether you work at home. Adjust the frequency of vacuuming to suit your home life.

Change the vacuum cleaner bag before it's completely full. Because full bags dump dirt everywhere, change the bag in the garage or outside to prevent the inevitable clouds of dust from spewing back into the air and onto your carpet, the floor, and the surrounding furniture.

Before changing the bag, run the vacuum on a clean floor for a few minutes. The vacuum inhales any remaining dirt in the hose so when you pull the bag, dirt doesn't spew back onto the floor.

Tape a reminder on the vacuum to change the belt two or three times a year, depending on the number of times you put the machine into action each week. Do this twice a year if you vacuum weekly, three times a year if you vacuum more frequently. Worn belts wear down motors quickly and prevent the beater from doing its job so the dirt stays trapped in your carpet.

Mary's Handy Hints

If your vacuum doesn't inhale dirt like it should, the bag might be full, the belt could be worn, or the beaters might have lint on them. If those are fine, remove the hose from the vacuum. Tape an old cotton tube sock to the end of a mop handle and run it through the hose to check for clogs. Still not working? Then it's time for a vacuum tune-up.

The Final Rinse

Whether you hire a professional carpet cleaner or rent a shampooer, carpet shampoo is going to leave a residue. Besides, most carpet shampoos are toxic, especially to children and pets.

Instead of shampoo, boil some water and add $\frac{1}{2}$ cup of white vinegar per gallon of water. Vinegar is not only a good cleaner, but also reactivates the shampoo already in your carpet and lifts it and the dirt out of the carpet. Your carpet will be clean and the fibers will be soft once more. Then clean with vinegar and water only for an inexpensive and toxic-free way to clean carpets.

Should you decide to hire a professional carpet cleaner, have them rinse the carpet with vinegar and hot water rather than plain water to lift the shampoo out of the carpet.

The Low-Down on Wood and Laminated Floors

Never use rubber-backed throw rugs on hard floor surfaces. They yellow the floor, which cannot be removed. Use a neutral-colored cotton throw rug with a separate nonslip pad. Remove the rug at night so the floor can breathe if you use a nonslip pad.

Homeowners love the look of hardwood floors because of their aged feel and sturdiness that brings back nostalgic days. But these floors are hard in name only.

Both hardwood and laminate floors scratch easily. Sweeping with a broom can scratch them if the broom picks up a pebble. Reach for a 100 percent cotton mop instead. The long strings keep stones and grit from scraping the floor. For large floor areas, visit a janitorial supply store and pick up a mightier dust mop for your home. Do not use a microfiber mop as it will ruin the floor.

Mary's Handy Hints

Wood floors will need to be sanded and refinished if they have been damaged by a liquid such as pet urine that went unnoticed. It's also time to break out the sander if the floor has dulled or the boards have warped from being mopped with excess water.

Some people recommend spraying a cotton dust mop with a dusting spray. Over time, the spray builds up and makes the floor slick. Worse, the spray can damage the floor. And worse still, the toxic spray lingers in the air and bioaccumulates in your body. If a spray sticks to a surface, it sticks to your lungs and organs, as well.

Lovin' Moppin'

Dusting floors is a breeze. Removing sticky stains might be a bit more work. Never use excess moisture on wood or laminate floors. Water works between the boards and they eventually warp.

Instead of slopping out water from a bucket, lightly spritz a terry cloth towel with a mixture $\frac{1}{4}$ cup white vinegar per quart of water. Mop the floor with this towel, shifting the towel as needed when the exposed section soils. The floor dries almost immediately, so you'll never need to dry it. For those sticky spots, spritz a bit of the vinegar and water on the spot, let it set a minute, and then rub it off with your toe on top of the towel.

Never wax a laminated floor and be very cautious with wood floors. Wax and cleaners other than vinegar can damage these floors. Follow the manufacturer's recommendations for wood floors.

> **Dirty Words**
> The vegetable soap used in Murphy's Oil Soap and similar products sticks to hardwood floors. Over time, it causes the sealant to become gummy. Eventually, the floor needs refinishing. You can't sand and refinish laminate flooring like you can wood floors. You must replace the entire floor!

Counting the Rings

Wood floors that are between 35 and 100 years old require different care than their newer cousins. You still must dust them weekly with a cotton dust mop. To clean up small spills, use the vinegar-and-water solution mentioned in the previous section.

To clean the floor, place the vinegar-and-water solution into a spray bottle and lightly spritz the cotton dust mop until it's barely dampened. Mop the floor and then launder the duster.

Treat older wood floors two or three times a year with paste wax to maintain their luster. Make sure the paste wax is designed for hardwood floors because not all waxes are created equal. Test a very small spot first for compatibility. You can wax small areas with a household buffer or a towel mop. For large surfaces, consider renting a buffing machine using only a lambswool wax applicator pad. Janitorial supply companies carry the pads.

For the Love of Linoleum

Use an angled nylon broom for sweeping linoleum floors. They angle into corners and don't shed the way *corn brooms* shed. Plus, they are better at picking up fine dust with less chance of scratching the floor. Make sure the broom has soft flagged ends.

Clean linoleum floors with a terry cloth towel and $1/4$ cup of white vinegar per gallon of hot water. If the floor has deep grooves that require additional cleaning, add two tablespoons of borax to this mixture. Scrub the floor with a soft nylon scrub brush. Never use a floor cleaner because many contain phosphorous or other heavy cleaners. They deteriorate the sealant and have been connected to serious health issues.

If your floor has dulled and is not coming clean, it could be time to strip and wax it. Purchase your floor stripper, sealant, and non-yellowing wax from a janitorial supply store. The supplies are more expensive but cost far less than replacing your floor. You will be well pleased with the lasting results.

Strip the floor following the bottle's directions. Rinse with $\frac{1}{2}$ cup vinegar per gallon of water. Apply the sealant, allow it to dry, and then add two coats of wax allowing the first coat to dry before applying the next layer. A sealer is necessary to obtain the proper waxing results.

def•i•ni•tion

A **corn broom** is made from a plant called broomcorn. Fully grown, the plant resembles field corn. The fibrous ends are tufted to make a corn broom. If you like this broom, purchase one made in the traditional way to prevent scratching the floor. You can find these at The North Woven Broom Co. (www. northwovenbroom.com or 1-866-471-1117)

Cork and Bamboo Rock and Roll

Cork floors are touted to be ecofriendly, low carbon, durable, warm, and easy to install and maintain. You must protect the floor from scratches by placing felt padding under furniture. Place mats at the door so you can remove your shoes and avoid scratching these floors. Clean them as you would a natural wood floor.

Bamboo floors dent easily, so you might want to think twice before installing bamboo. Never use moisture on a bamboo floor because you can warp the floor. Spot clean only. This is not a floor for a home with kids or pets. Both cork and bamboo floors fade, especially in the sun.

Marble, Slate, Granite, and Tile Floors

To prevent scratches on granite and marble floors, use only a cotton dust mop. You need nothing more than hot water to clean stone floors. Any kind of detergent or vinegar pits these floors. Detergents seep into the pores of tile floors causing a sticky buildup that attracts dirt and is difficult to remove so the floor always looks dirty. Over time, the detergent softens the adhesive on the back of the tile, causing it to loosen.

To clean granite and marble floors, mop a small section and then immediately dry it because these floors water spot easily. These water spots are difficult to remove. Immediately wipe spills.

Grout stains can be stubborn to remove. Grout is porous, so cleaners soak right through and strip the color out of colored grout. Use sudsy water and a toothbrush, or try The StainEraser. Appendix B tells you where to buy them. Seal your grout after cleaning it by applying a five-year grout sealer. Wait three to four days and seal it again. Purchase a syringe for large animals from a western feed store. Remove the needle and fill the syringe with sealer for an easy applicator.

We find it faster to vacuum tile or slate floors than sweeping them. Mop them with hot water only and use a terry towel. Like granite and marble, dry ceramic tile to prevent streaking.

The Least You Need to Know

- Place area rugs or matting on hard floor surfaces, especially wood, to keep them clean longer and help prevent scratches and mars.

- Kick your shoes off when you enter your home and you won't need to clean the carpet so often.

- Keep from warping your wood floors by using as little water as possible.

- Vinegar and water work well on vinyl and linoleum to keep those surfaces looking great; add just a bit of borax if needed.

- The only things that should go on a stone or tile floor are your feet and hot water; detergents damage them, as does vinegar.

Chapter 11

Walls, Ceilings, and Windows

In This Chapter

- ◆ Up against the wall
- ◆ Tricks for tricky ceilings
- ◆ Pro secrets of streak-free windows
- ◆ Fireplace know-how

Everything in your home sparkles after reading the last 10 chapters, right? Just don't look up, straight ahead, or down near your feet. We're talking ceilings, windows, walls, and baseboards. Those areas where if we remove our glasses, we can't see the dirt. If we can't see it, then we don't have to clean it.

Not quite. You need to clean these areas—unless you like hanging out with dust mites and cobwebs, and all the sneezing and wheezing and possible lung problems that come with them. Spiders hold a three-ring circus on your ceilings, leaving their "tents" behind while your artistically talented children redecorate the walls with crayons. All the while, a good north wind plasters the windows with more than a bit of dirt.

With the handy tips in this chapter, you'll be fitting these chores into your regular cleaning regimen.

Ceiling Cleaning

When it comes to cleaning tricky surfaces like textured walls or "popcorn" ceilings, it sometimes seems necessary to pull magical tricks out of a hat. When you finish reading the tricks in this section, you'll have the magic—all you add is the equipment and the arm motion (a.k.a. elbow grease). No, Mary doesn't make house calls anymore, unless you live in the outback of Alaska and promise to take her salmon fishing!

Your goal is to not only rid walls and ceilings of dirt, but also rid your life of toxic chemicals. If the ailments mentioned in Chapter 2 caused by some of these cleaners were not enough to get you to switch, let's take a look at one of the most frequently used cleaners for ceilings and walls.

Dirty Words

When you clean walls and ceilings, stay away from any product that leaves a gummy residue on the walls. This residue prevents paint from sticking even five years down the road, leaving you with a miserable mess.

Tri-sodium phosphate (TSP) is often recommended for cleaning walls and ceilings and even recommended by many "green" sites as safe to use. It causes severe eye and skin irritations, asthma, as well as lung and intestinal track irritations. Continued use can permanently scar eye and membrane tissue.

Remember: Never spray a cleaner on overhead surfaces like ceilings and walls. It doesn't matter if the cleaner is green or not because your body cannot process chemicals and they can damage organs. Dip your cloth or sponge in the cleaner; then wipe it on the wall or ceiling. Here are some green ways to clean these areas.

Flat or Painted

Follow these steps to clean ceilings, which may stall the need to paint for several years:

1. Remove all wall hangings, curtains, and blinds. Move furniture to one side of the room; then lay down a canvas drop cloth. Plastic can get slippery when wet, so use precautions when using it. If you use plastic, cover it with towels to catch the drips and be careful out there!

2. Mix 1 cup of borax into a gallon of water, and then add $\frac{1}{4}$ cup of organic laundry detergent. Do not use essential oils on walls or ceilings.

3. Clean one section at a time doing the ceiling first and then the wall. Clean the ceiling and walls using a towel draped over a towel mop. If you are going to repaint, a microfiber mop will also work.

4. Rinse the ceiling as you clean with a gallon of water plus $\frac{1}{2}$ cup of white vinegar. Dry immediately.

If you just want to remove cobwebs, use a barely damp towel over a towel mop or a lambswool duster. People also vacuum cobwebs so clean them with whatever method is easiest and fastest for you.

Now you can look up at your beautiful ceiling!

Popcorn, Textured, or Wood Beam

To clean popcorn ceilings and wood beams, slip three lint-remover replacement tubes over the metal base of a paint roller. Attach the roller to your extension handle and roll the ceiling or wood beams to remove dust and cobwebs without smearing the cobwebs or scattering spackling compound everywhere. Duct tape the end of the paint roller to protect the walls from being marred.

Cleaning the Walls

If dirty walls are, well, driving you up the wall, then keep reading. Try the green way to removing snafus from walls:

◆ Remove small marks by rubbing gently with an art gum eraser.

◆ No art gum eraser on hand? Rub the mark gently with toothpaste. Rinse with mouthwash and floss. (We are kidding about the mouthwash but the toothpaste works!)

♦ Pour a few tablespoons of baking soda into a small container and add enough hydrogen peroxide to make a paste. Apply and let it set for five minutes; this will "bubble" off the stain. Then gently blot with a clean cloth.

♦ To remove ink, gently use an art gum eraser. If that fails, blot the inside or zest of a lemon or an orange peel on the spot and rub gently. Wait 10 minutes and gently blot to remove it.

Tackling Tougher Stains

If you're dealing with stains from grease, oil, or crayons, well, that's a tougher cookie to chew.

> **Dirty Words**
>
> Never use mineral spirits, liquid dish soaps, or WD-40 to remove grease or oil. These products leave a sticky residue, which causes the paint to turn gummy the next time you paint. They are toxic, except for organic dish soap, so you not only breathe the fumes but also absorb the toxins through your hands.

Most stains come right out by dampening a cloth with warm water and pouring a bit of organic laundry powder or liquid detergent on the cloth. Borax works well, too. Blot to remove. If that fails, try this:

1. Mix a tablespoon or two of cornstarch and enough water to make a thick paste.

2. Plaster the spot and let the mixture dry several hours. As the cornstarch dries, it will absorb the oil.

3. Brush off the cornstarch with a paint brush and wipe off any residue with a barely damp cotton cloth.

4. See Appendix A for specific stain remedies.

If the grease decides to be as stubborn as a Missouri mule, you'll have to apply a water-based primer over the grease and then paint the area using some leftover wall paint.

Mary's Handy Hints _____

You might need to add a bit of black paint to darken your leftover wall paint to blend it to the right color. Remove a small amount of paint from the can and place it on a piece of waxed paper. Use a flat toothpick to retrieve a dab of black paint. Mix until you have a reasonable match for the paint.

Washing the Walls

Refer to the section "Ceiling Cleaning," earlier in this chapter, for general wall washing directions.

- **Sponge them.** Always wash your walls with a natural sponge, found in paint stores. Rags, towels, and flat mops can take the paint off flat wall paints. They can be used on gloss or semi-gloss paints; just don't aggressively clean them.

Mary's Handy Hints _____

Cut the foot off a clean but old cotton tube sock and place the sock over your wrist to catch the dripping water before it runs down your arms. Use the foot section for polishing shoes.

- **Go in order.** Most experts tell you to wash from the top down to avoid the dirt streaks that drip down from the top. Never clean walls from the bottom up unless you like recleaning the bottom area as the water drips from the top.

We have a neat trick that will solve the drippy problem: when washing walls up high, cover a dust pan with a hand-size terry cloth towel and hold it just under the area you're cleaning to catch those drips.

Wash the wall from right to left and left to right in the same direction paint is applied. Cleaning in a circular motion goes against the grain of the paint, which can leave it scratched.

Rinse walls using a second bucket of water plus $\frac{1}{2}$ cup of white vinegar per gallon of water, and dry immediately. Vinegar is an excellent cleaner and has the ability to remove a cleaner from the wall, so paint glides on easily.

Even if you are using a green cleaner, open the windows and doors and turn on a fan to circulate the fumes out of your home. Spring and fall are the best times of year for heavier cleaning chores because the doors and windows are usually open anyway.

Treating Paneling

The popular wood paneling of the '70s has, unfortunately, made a comeback. Cutting down trees to line our walls is difficult for me to bear since so much of our vital forests are being needlessly destroyed simply for our "viewing" pleasure. Please think twice before paneling your home. Let's go clean them.

All wood paneling, whether it's synthetic, finished, or raw wood, must be dusted regularly. Use a wool duster, dry sponge, or barely damp cotton terry towel over a towel mop to dust.

Follow the instructions for your type of wood paneling:

◆ **Unfinished wood paneling.** Lightly wipe clean using a barely damp cloth. Excess moisture on unfinished wood paneling can damage the wood. Wait 24 hours and then apply a wood treatment recommended by the manufacturer.

◆ **Sealed or finished wood paneling.** Generally, damp cleaning finished paneling isn't necessary. A dry sponge should remove most surface dirt.

 Dirty Words

Please heed all prior warnings concerning the use of petroleum distillates-based products inside the home. Also stay away from linseed oil as well. Linseed oil, in large enough amounts to treat paneling, will overwhelm you with fumes and cause severe headaches. Linseed oil spontaneously combusts catching a rag and your home on fire. A beeswax-based conditioner does a safe job cleaning and conditioning paneling.

If grime has developed on the paneling, clean it with a solution of $\frac{1}{2}$ cup of white vinegar per gallon of water or a cleaner recommended by the manufacturer.

Work from the bottom up, cleaning with the grain of the wood. As the dry sponge soils, take it outside and sand it with 600- to 800-grit fine sandpaper.

If you need to wash the paneling, use a damp cloth and work from the bottom upward. Why bottom up here but top down for painted walls? On finished wood, any dirty water dripping down could streak the finish, and the streaks are difficult to remove. Hold a terry towel under the spot you are cleaning to catch drips.

Fireplace Fronts

The plastic is down and cleaning equipment out, so why not tackle the fireplace front too? Be sure to cover the base of the fireplace and the carpet with one piece of plastic. Liquids can seep through overlapping plastic and stain the carpet:

1. Head to a janitorial supply store for what is called a foaming sprayer. Get two of them in case one breaks. Saturate the bricks with the heaviest dilution of your green cleaner, adding a few drops of pine oil. Wait a few minutes.

2. Using the foaming sprayer, add $2/3$ cup borax and $1/3$ cup of a green laundry detergent per gallon of your cleaner. Thoroughly spray the bricks or stones. The foaming sprayer foams the cleaner, which then "foams" the soot out of the bricks.

3. Scrub using a stiff bristle brush dipped in the cleaning solution. Reapply as needed.

Keep the room well ventilated and wear gloves and a mask. Even though you are using green cleaners, you are working in a tight area around the fireplace.

Window Wizardry

If your windows give you a crystal-clear view, congratulations! They are clean and you can kick your feet up and laugh at the rest of us who are dragging out the ladders.

Dirty Words

Paper towels and newspaper contain pieces of pulp that scratch glass. Use lint-free towels and wash them first adding white vinegar to the rinse cycle. Vinegar removes any soap residue that can smear glass. Dry them using no dryer sheets.

Grandmother had many words of wisdom, but don't adopt Grandma's use of crumpled newspaper. Instead, follow these professional tips for squeaky clean windows.

Whenever possible, avoid spraying even your home-brew window cleaner directly on glass. Those droplets float down so you inhale them the entire time you clean windows. Instead, dampen the Window Scrubber from The Clean Team or a cotton scrubber from a hardware store and then clean the window.

From the Inside Out

Cleaning the inside of windows is much easier than the outside, so let's tackle that first. Mix a batch of window cleaner following the recipe given in Chapter 4. Use distilled water as it gives the best results, or try Benya or the Blue Juice from The Clean Team.

Clear the windowsills and push aside the curtains. Hold one lint-free towel over a sheet of plastic laid on the floor and lightly spray the cleaner on the towel. Wipe over the window; then dry with a second 100 percent cotton lint-free towel. Windows, except for tinted ones, are the one surface where you have our permission to use microfiber products—vehicle windshields are the other. Microfiber will not scratch glass since it does not have a coating. It scratches plastic, so keep it off plastic and Plexiglas skylights.

Lay a towel on the windowsill to catch any drips. Finally, step back and look through windows so crystal clear you don't know they're there.

From the Outside In

Outside windows take a beating. From rain pounding on the panes to dust and dirt and even birds flying into the glass, outside windows require more effort to get them clean.

You may be using a squeegee to clean outside windows. Clean the rubber blade with soap and water to remove any manufacturing oil left on the rubber. Otherwise, they can streak the window.

Of course, you need to remove the screens first and clean them. You are going to love this quick trick to clean screens. Rather than washing screens and all the other nonsense you go through, grab a dry sponge and wipe them front and back. Sand the sponge as it soils with a 600- to 800-grit sandpaper.

Mary's Handy Hints

No matter which type of glass cleaner you use, cleaning your windows in the morning or early evening gives you the best results. When glass becomes hot from the sun's rays, the window cleaner dries too quickly, leaving it streaked.

Clean aluminum frames with a metal polish such as the one from The Clean Team, or Mary Moppins and rinse with a damp cloth. For painted frames, clean with your organic cleaner and a damp cloth.

Brush the windowsills and framing with a medium-size paintbrush to remove bits of leaves and other debris. Clean the sills and framing with your organic cleaner or metal polish if they are aluminum.

To clean the windows themselves, you'll want to take a page from the professionals and use a squeegee, a lint-free towel, and some quick wrist action. Here are the steps:

1. Mix together 1 tablespoon of organic, powdered dishwashing detergent and $\frac{1}{2}$ cup of white vinegar in a bucket of water.

2. Using a cloth-headed window squeegee or a lint-free towel, swab the solution on the window from top to bottom.

3. Use the rubber blade of the squeegee to wipe off the solution. Start by using one corner of the blade to wipe where the top edge of the window meets the frame.

4. Continue down the window working right to left so that the squeegee pushes water down as you move across the glass. Overlap the strokes by an inch so you leave no water behind. At the end of each stroke, wipe the squeegee dry with a cloth.

5. Remove any remaining water on the sides of the glass with a lint-free towel or a microfiber cloth.

6. Dry the window frame and sill with a separate rag—not the lint-free towel. If the frame is aluminum, clean it with a metal polish like Met-All or The Clean Team's Stainless Steel polish to prevent corrosion. This also helps the window to slide easier as well.

First time wielding a squeegee? You may find you leave a few streaks behind before you pick up on the technique. You'll catch on quickly.

After you've finished washing the windows, park yourself in a chair in front of a picture window and enjoy the view!

The Least You Need to Know

◆ Always protect the floors and furniture before washing walls, ceilings, or windows and have all your cleaning products on hand.

◆ Remove marks from walls with an art gum eraser, toothpaste, or baking soda mixed with hydrogen peroxide.

◆ Clean popcorn ceilings and wood beams with lint-remover replacement tubes on a paint roller.

◆ When washing outside windows, forget the crumpled newspaper and do it like a pro—with a squeegee.

Chapter 12

The Great Green Outdoors

In This Chapter

- ◆ De-gunking gutters
- ◆ Cleaning the siding
- ◆ Manning the deck (and the patio)
- ◆ Sitting pretty on patio furniture

Remember in school how your teachers encouraged you to be well-rounded? They coaxed the athletes and computer whizzes to run for office or join the debate team.

Your home needs that well-rounded touch, too. So far this book has been a bit introverted sticking to inside cleaning issues. But the dirt on the outside of your home detracts from that inside sparkle. Besides, outside dirt always figures out how to hitch a ride into your home.

Grab your brush, ladder, and a bucket of water and follow us outside for some fresh air and—okay—some work as well.

Keep Your Siding in Check

Nature's elements break down that tough exterior surface making it a vulnerable target for dirt, mold, and other unsavory characters. Trust us; it's easier to clean siding before the mold starts building than wait until mold has moved inside.

Prevent Mold and Mildew

Left unchecked, mold can contaminate your entire home. Heavy rains and humidity start mold growing on the roof, siding, sidewalk, and driveway. Shoes carry mold spores inside where they become airborne and are carried throughout the entire home by the duct system. Inside mold pollution is difficult and costly to treat. That seems like an excellent argument in favor of kicking the habit of wearing shoes inside your home.

People usually reach for a bottle of bleach to kill mold and mildew. Let's take a look at a few "green" solutions.

Never allow a small mold infestation to grow into a large problem. Treat each spot when it first appears to prevent it from spreading. Scrub the spot using a brush and ½ cup of borax per gallon of water to remove the mold. Let that dry. Using a sponge, wipe on straight white vinegar and let it dry. If the mold remains, treat it with 35 percent food-grade hydrogen peroxide. Repeat at the first sign of new mold growth.

Treat larger areas with a mixture of ½ cup borax, ⅔ cup organic cleaner, and 32 ounces of white vinegar poured into a gallon of water. Scrub the area with a brush. After it dries, spray the siding with three parts vinegar to five parts water.

Aluminum and Vinyl Siding

Aluminum siding is a factory-painted metal that can oxidize or turn chalky if not properly cleaned. *Vinyl* siding etches over the years, making it prone to stains and dulling. Proper cleaning keeps you ahead of these problems.

Wash either siding with a long-handled, soft bristle brush. Use $\frac{1}{3}$ cup of an organic non-sudsing laundry detergent such as Bi-O-Kleen's laundry detergent or The Clean Team's Red Juice adding $\frac{1}{2}$ to 1 cup of distilled vinegar per bucket of water to retard mold growth. Be sure to turn off the electrical connection to any outdoor plugs before you begin. Start at the bottom and work your way to the top. Clean a section and then thoroughly rinse it.

Check with the siding manufacturer before you pressure wash siding. Some siding cannot be pressure washed. Set the pressure washer to the lowest setting and keep the nozzle two feet from the surface. Never aim the power washer upward because you can drive water behind the siding, which causes indoor mold problems.

Stucco

Stucco turns dark with accumulated dirt and mold. Both stucco and brick turn white with *efflorescence*. Clean stucco once a year, or twice a year if it's light in color.

def•i•ni•tion

Efflorescence occurs when the mineral salts in the mortar of your stucco dissolve. It leaves a white appearance that stands out from the rest of the stucco.

Stucco Cleaner

2 gallons hot water

$\frac{1}{4}$ cup organic laundry detergent (try the one by Bi-O-Kleen)

$\frac{1}{2}$ cup borax

$\frac{1}{2}$ cup washing soda

Mix together the above ingredients. If you are using a power washer, spray the dirt starting at the top and don't stop until you reach the bottom of that strip. If you stop, the grunge will stain the stucco. Keep the pressure set low; otherwise, you will knock the stucco off the side.

Brick

Exterior brick maintains its beauty with a simple yearly hosing. If you spot moss, mold, or mildew, thoroughly wet the brick with water. Next, scrub with a solution of 1 cup of 35 percent food-grade hydrogen peroxide per 1 gallon of water and a soft bristled brush. Never use a wire brush as it will damage the bricks.

Wood

Wood siding looks great, although it is high maintenance. Paint or stain it every five years to protect it. Keep it beautiful longer by cleaning it twice a year.

Pressure wash wood siding with the nozzle set to the lowest setting. Alternatively, use a soft brush and $\frac{1}{2}$ cup powdered laundry detergent and $\frac{1}{3}$ cup borax per bucket of water.

De-Gunk the Gutters

You can't help but wonder if gutters don't get a chuckle out of trapping leaves so they can laugh at the strange positions you engage trying to clean them. If they aren't laughing, the neighbors certainly are. Gutters protect your home by directing rain away from your siding, doors, windows, and foundation. They keep your home dry!

You need to clean (and repair, if necessary) gutters twice a year. Here's what you need to get started:

- Rubber work gloves and safety glasses
- Gutter scoop (found at hardware stores) and a ladder
- Gutter seal and plumber's snake
- Water hose with a high-pressure nozzle
- Chalk and caulking gun

Dirty Words

Never lean your ladder against the gutter unless you like damaged gutters. Gutter attachments found at hardware stores let you raise the ladder higher than the gutter without damaging it.

Ladder Safety

Don't risk an accident to clean gutters. (No, I am not giving you permission to skip cleaning them!) Always make sure your ladder is firmly anchored. If you'll be using an extension ladder rather than a step ladder, have someone hold the ladder.

Wear heavy work gloves to protect your hands against screws or sharp metal bits on the trough. Wear heavy-duty shoes like boat deck shoes or rubber boots that give you good traction. Hiking or outdoor shoes throw you off balance because the soles are not flat and often have ridges that catch on ladder steps.

Where to Start

What's holding you up? Let's get those gutters cleaned:

1. Before you start, use a strap or hook to hang a bucket from the ladder to collect debris. Begin at the drain outlet at the low end of the gutter and scoop to the other end of your home using the gutter scoop.

2. Hose out the gutters starting at the opposite end of the drain outlet working toward the outlet. Stubborn dirt can be persuaded to come loose with a stiff scrub brush.

3. Drainpipes plugged? Stick the power nozzle down the pipe and turn on the water full blast. You may need to use a plumber's snake to pull out debris. Push the snake up the pipe from the bottom until you unclog the drain. Keep a screen over the pipe opening to keep out drain-clogging leaves.

4. As you hose the drain, have someone on the ground watch for water leaks in the seams. Mark the leaks with chalk. Let the gutters dry and then seal them with gutter seal. The next day spray water down the gutter to make sure they are sealed.

5. While you are on the ladder, look behind the gutter for daylight. If you see daylight, the gutter has separated from the house. Pull out the loose spikes and replace them with gutter bolts from the hardware store.

6. The outside of the gutters need cleaning too! Mix $1/3$ cup of powdered laundry detergent and $1/2$ cup of borax in a gallon of water. Add 2 cups of hydrogen peroxide if mold or mildew is pesky. Wear gloves and then scrub them with a white scrub pad. Use only white scrub pads as the other colors scratch the gutter.

All Hands on Deck

We all love sitting on the deck sipping a cool lemonade while reading a good book. Don't look down or the dirt and grime on the deck might lay a guilt trip on you until you clean it.

Give deck dirt the brush-off with these tips:

◆ Organic matter such as leaves, maple seeds (helicopter seeds), and twigs can stain your deck. Sweep such debris off the deck frequently.

◆ If you can't see it, it won't hurt your deck, right? Good try—but wrong. Debris builds up between the boards trapping moisture. Then mold starts growing and the boards rot. Run a spade or a wallboard spackling trowel (even an old spatula works) between the boards to knock down the debris. Water is a precious resource so save Mother Earth and don't use the hose.

◆ Gas grills are awesome for serving up burgers, but their grease stains are not so awesome on the deck. Place an aluminum pan used for protecting floors from car grease under your grill.

Keep reading to learn the specific care for each deck.

Cleaning Redwood or Cedar Decks

If you don't mind the grayish hue of redwood or cedar decks, rinse the deck and scrub it with a stiff-bristle brush. To bring the luster back, apply a deck brightener found at home centers.

Cleaning Pressure-Treated Pine Decks

Clean pressure-treated decks with a solution of $\frac{1}{2}$ cup borax and $\frac{1}{3}$ cup powdered organic laundry soap per gallon of water. Or blast away dirt with a power washer set on medium.

Patio

You need to clean your patio without turning the surrounding shrubs and flowers into yard waste after using toxic cleaners on the patio. We have an ecofriendly solution. For concrete patios, mix a solution of 1 gallon of warm water, 1 cup of white vinegar, and 2 tablespoons of borax. Hose down the patio and pour on some of the solution scrubbing with a long-handled brush. Make sure you thoroughly rinse the patio including the surrounding yard. Tile and stone patios can be scrubbed with an organic cleaner and a scrub brush. Rinse thoroughly.

Borax also kills fleas, ants, and cockroaches so leave them some powdered "food" when you finish the patio. Keep children and pets away from treated areas until it has dried.

Patio Furniture

The great outdoors is filled with fresh air, beautiful trees, our four-legged friends, the winged ones in the sky—and don't forget dirt. Translation? Clean the patio furniture every season.

Plastic Furniture

Clean plastic furniture, but forget about removing stains. They don't come out even with extreme elbow grease. You can paint it with paint made for plastic furniture. Clean the furniture using your organic general-duty cleaner. Follow the can's directions to paint—be sure to lay down fabric drop cloths. Avoid plastic tarps because they do not biodegrade and leave lasting footprints.

Wicker Furniture

Use a paintbrush or a soft-bristle brush from a vacuum cleaner to remove dust and cobwebs on wicker furniture.

Clean your wicker furniture four times a year with two drops of organic liquid dish soap in a bucket of water. Dampen a soft cloth—not a terry towel—in the bucket and wipe to clean. Soap and water prevent wicker from drying and cracking.

Mary's Handy Hints

Cut off 1 inch of a 2-inch-wide paintbrush to clean the crevices of wicker furniture that the vacuum cleaner won't reach. After cutting off the top of the paintbrush, the bristles are stiffer and work into the wicker more easily than soft bristles.

Wrought-Iron Furniture

To remove dust and dirt, first use the soft-bristle brush of your vacuum cleaner and then switch to a paintbrush as suggested previously. If the furniture has begun to rust, switch to a wire brush and scrub it good. Then clean with a stiff-bristle brush and air dry. Paint it with rust-resistant paint.

Mary's Handy Hints

A protective coat of liquid beeswax or shellac on your wrought iron retards rusting and simplifies cleaning jobs.

Clean wrought-iron furniture with ionized water. It's expensive, but you only need a cup or two. Chemicals in water damage wrought iron, and ionized water prevents it from rusting. Use a wet or dry vacuum to inhale the water as you clean.

Aluminum Framing Furniture

Metal polish such as Met-All, The Clean Team's Stainless Steel Cleaner, or AlumiBrite by Mary Moppins cleans and polishes non-painted aluminum framing. Clean aluminum twice a year to retard oxidation. A 50/50 solution of white vinegar to water and a good nylon scrub brush clean aluminum but will not remove the oxidation that dulls the finish.

Clean painted metal framing with 1 tablespoon of concentrated organic cleaner per bucket of warm water. If you're really energetic, a toothbrush cleans the small crevices quite nicely.

Fabric and Vinyl Cushions

Clean fabric cushions and pads with a tablespoon of organic cleaner and 2 drops essential pine oil per gallon of water. Wipe on the surface, wait 10 to 15 minutes, then rinse with ½ cup of white vinegar per gallon of water. Air dry.

Tree sap sticking around? First freeze it with an ice cube. Chip off what you can with the blunt side of a kitchen knife. Then dab on a bit of creamy peanut butter to remove the rest. Wait several minutes and clean with sudsy water. Always test an area first, as the peanut butter can stain.

Patio Umbrellas

Open the umbrella and brush off all the dust and dirt. Then remove any sap with ice and peanut butter as described previously. Using a foam sprayer from a janitorial supply store, spray the umbrella with your organic cleaner. Add 4–5 drops of an essential oil like pine. Start at the bottom, working your way to the hole at the top. Grab a white scrub pad, add a bit of elbow grease, and clean the surface. Rinse with a solution of ½ cup white vinegar per gallon of water. Dry in the sun.

Cement Surfaces

Your yard and home should be ready for the cover of *Home Beautiful* by now, right? That is, as long as you don't check out the mold covered driveway or the sidewalk full of weeds growing between the cracks. Caring for these areas without damaging either our Mother Earth, ruining your health, or wiping out the surrounding grass and shrubs can be tricky. Here are safe, ecofriendly ways to take care of these sore spots.

Sweep, Don't Hose

Take a walk through any neighborhood on the weekend and a dozen or more people will be hosing a few leaves into the street. A hose not only takes longer to clean the driveway than a broom, but also wastes gallons of precious water.

Many areas of our country are under heavy drought conditions. Conserve the water, push a broom, and get your heart rate going and your blood circulating. If physical problems prevent this kind of exercise, then hire a neighbor's child.

Remove the Mold and Mildew

When you see black before your eyes after sweeping the driveway, it's time to rent a pressure washer, which is the most effective method to clean concrete surfaces. Set the pressure on the lowest possible setting that will effectively remove mold and dirt. Use care along the sides where grass and shrubs can easily be damaged.

Aim the nozzle into crevices to remove mold growing in those spots. After you finish, mix a solution of 50/50 water to white vinegar. Pour the solution in the crevices to kill any mold spores that might still be hanging around. Just be careful not to get any on shrubs, grass, or flowers. It will kill them as well.

After treating the crevices, start at the top of the driveway and gently pour some of the solution on the driveway. A gallon-size watering can works well for this. Using a push broom, sweep it to the end of the driveway. Repeat this twice a year to keep mold from returning. Add ½ cup of borax to clean the cement; then you never have to power wash.

Grease and Oil Be Gone

One of your out-of-town friends stopped by on his way through town and left a gift of oil in your driveway.

Whenever you work on your car, always place a flat pan found at an automotive store under the car to catch drips. For fresh spills, immediately grab some old rags and absorb as much oil as possible. Store the rags in an open plastic bag; then take them to the toxic waste dump for proper disposal. Do not leave these rags lying around because they can spontaneously combust.

After absorbing as much oil as possible with rags, pour kitty litter or sawdust on the spot and let it absorb the oil overnight. Sweep to remove; then pour dry cement on the spot to absorb the rest.

The Least You Need to Know

◆ Check with your siding manufacturer before you clean it.

◆ Always use safety precautions and wear nonskid shoes when working on a ladder.

◆ Clean your deck, patio, and patio furniture once a year to keep them mold and dirt free.

◆ Never use any kind of cleaner outdoors unless you have read the MSDS sheet and know it is safe for Mother Earth.

Chapter 13

Mean Green Driving Machines

In This Chapter

- ◆ TLCC—Tender Loving Car Care
- ◆ Times have changed, and so have vehicle paints
- ◆ Keep those tires spinning round and round
- ◆ The good, the shiny, and the ugly sides of waxes

Signs and billboards along our nation's highways are often humorous and sometimes ill placed. One such ill-placed sign is a plug for California farmers along I5 that says "California farmers clean the air with the crops they grow." That area of California grows almonds and fruit. Trees have long been known for their ability to cleanse the air of toxins. The problem is that the sign is placed directly in front of a large and odorous dairy farm, so it loses just a bit of its believability.

A bumper sticker in Arizona reads "A woman's place is in the House and Senate" and another on a rather old beat-up truck in Wyoming states "If it's got tires it's gonna give you trouble."

The information in this chapter will help keep your tires out of trouble while the cleaning guidelines won't foul up the environment with toxins. Besides, your vehicle will end up so shiny you'll use it to taxi Congresspersons around town.

Washing Cars, Vans, Trucks, RVs, Trailers, and Boats

By now you may be wondering what a home cleaning expert could possibly know about caring for cars, boats, or RVs. Maybe she could remove a carpet stain, but tires and waxes? When Mary started selling her products to RVers, she was asked to present cleaning seminars during which people asked questions about things called holding tanks and rubber roofs.

Because Mary knew nothing about cleaning these items and folks needed their problems solved, she started calling manufacturers to learn the proper care for the various parts of an RV. She spoke and met personally with the companies who manufacture the rubber roofing, fiberglass and metal bodies, tires, and paint.

She then applied her professional cleaning knowledge to the problem areas and developed cleaning solutions that protect the surfaces rather than damage it. Over time and hard earned trust, major RV magazine editors requested cleaning articles. Her seminars are now backed and approved by major RV motorhome manufacturers. So, grab a bucket and let's put a shine on those vehicles.

We all learned to wash our cars from our parents, who dragged out a bottle of liquid dishwashing detergent and poured enough in the bucket to clean five months' worth of dishes. Times have changed, and so have both the formulas for dish soaps and paint. (The next section brings you current on paint issues.)

Most paint manufacturers recommend using mild soap and not degreasing cleaners like orange-based cleaners, cleaners made for removing grease and oil, liquid dish soaps, and even ecofriendly degreasing agents. The reason? The job of these cleaners is to break down grease, oil, and heavy dirt. Over time they also break down the clear and gel coat finish on a vehicle, boat, or RV. Given sufficient time, the paint starts to oxidize because the protective coating has been weakened.

You have read my raves on using white vinegar for cleaning. Well, it does a great job cleaning vehicles as well. It neutralizes the alkaline in water to help prevent water spots. It also boosts the cleaning ability of a cleaner—if you need one at all.

Unless the vehicle is quite dirty, all you need to wash is $\frac{1}{3}$ cup vinegar per gallon of water. Up that to $\frac{1}{2}$ cup if your water is hard. For extra dirty vehicles, add half a capful of an ecofriendly baby shampoo that does not contain sodium laurel sulfate or dioxide.

You will read articles saying not to use an acid to wash a vehicle. Vinegar is an acid, but it's a natural acid made from grain. These articles are speaking about muratic or phosphoric acids, which will destroy a paint job and are highly toxic.

Dirty Words

Degreasing cleaners also soften the adhesive holding decals, striping, and lettering to the side of any vehicle, trailer, boat, or airplane. When that adhesive softens, the decal, stripping, and lettering pull away from the surface.

Dirty Words

Resist the temptation to use a product like Rain Ex or wax on your vehicle windshields. If a rock chips the glass and you need to have it repaired, the repair material will not stick to Rain Ex. You will eventually have to replace the windshield.

The oil buildup around the exhaust of boats usually requires a heavier cleaner like The Clean Team's Red Juice or CleanEz. Dampen a towel and pour a bit of cleaner on your towel; then wipe it down. Wait a few minutes and add a bit of elbow grease and rinse thoroughly.

Remember to immediately clean bugs and bird droppings off the front of your vehicle and any paint. Bugs and bird droppings have an acid that will eat through paint if left on for even a few days. Later you might think they are rock chips, but that is bug or bird "juice" that has eaten away the paint.

Volatile Organic Compounds (VOCs) and Paint

So what's the big fuss about paint and picking on certain cleaners? Travel back in time to 1978 when the government banned the use of lead in house paint and paint used on toys due to the large number of children being poisoned by lead paint. By the early 1990s, awareness began rising over the toxins emitted by lead at paint manufacturing plants. Finally, lead was removed from all paint, including that used for vehicles.

That meant changing the paint base. There are dozens of bases for paint; the two most common are water- or chroma-based paints. In the "good ole days," if a detergent was used on lead paint, it took 10 years or longer for the paint to show signs of *oxidation*. Then it took another 2 years before the paint oxidized to the point of needing a new paint job.

def•i•ni•tion

When **oxidation** occurs on a painted vehicle surface, the paint "sheds" its color. Eventually, the paint becomes splotchy white and disappears completely causing the frame to rust.

A water- or chroma-based paint is a soft base. A heavy-duty cleaner or degreasing agent can deteriorate this paint within a few short years.

Trouble in Brush Land

Wait a minute—you used this same brush on your old vehicle for years and now it has left nasty brush marks on your new car. Brushes don't come with warning buzzers that sound when they need replacing. Those flagged ends break down over time leaving nasty scratches on your vehicle's surface. Plus, the paint on new vehicles is softer and scratches easily.

The only 100 percent safe brush for vehicles Mary recommends is made from boar's hair. Otherwise, stay a step ahead of the problem and replace your brush every two years. Use a marker to note the purchase date on the brush so you know when to replace it.

Heed Mary's warnings about microfiber and how it scratches surfaces over time. The same applies for any vehicle surface, including cars, semi trucks, vans, trailers, airplanes, boats, and motorcycles. It may take several years for the damage to rear its ugly head, but it will—and a new paint job is expensive.

Mary's Handy Hints

Boar's hair brushes are difficult to find. Because they are expensive, most automotive supply stores don't carry them. You can find a good one online called the Montana Original Boar's Hair Brush. Several online detail shops also carry this brush.

The paint manufacturers Mary consults recommend 100 percent lambswool or cotton wash mitts or pads. Be cautious of imitation lambswool because it is 100 percent polyester, the same material as microfiber.

Tire Care

Tires are good for a few things. They get you where you want to go and they make great tree swings or sand lots for the kids.

Tire manufacturers recommend scrubbing tires four times a year with laundry soap, water, and a tire brush. Rubber naturally oxidizes, which makes a tire look like it's drying out. Scrubbing removes the oxidation and prevents drying. If a vehicle like an RV or show car sits for long periods of time, be sure to drive it 100 miles each month. Tires are self-lubricating. Driving brings the natural oil to the surface to keep them lubricated.

You do not need a treatment on tires. Yes, you like the shiny look, but eventually you are going to see that shiny look scattered all over the road. The petroleum distillates in most tire treatments make them shine but it disintegrates the rubber causing them to blow out. Besides, they are extremely toxic to our Earth and you.

If your tire does blow out and is under warranty, you just lost the warranty. Warranties only protect against manufacturing defects. If you have been using a treatment, the tire company will rightfully blame the treatment and not replace the tire. If you use a treatment, keep your spare tire inflated.

Whether a wheel is aluminum, plastic, or sealed, wash them with organic soap and water. Head into a hardware store and purchase some sponge paint brushes. They are small and flexible and clean easily around the rims, nuts, and brake holes.

Clean aluminum wheels with a metal polish like Flitz, Met-All, or Mary's AlumiBrite. Polishes remove brake dust and oxidation—and, boy, do they shine. Never use a metal polish on plastic or sealed wheels even if the polish says it's safe. They will scratch off the sealant. To tell whether a wheel is sealed, look for the identification number. Sealed wheels have the letter "C" at the end of the number.

Wash Towels the Right Way

You have been washing towels a long time and don't need some lady coming along telling you how to do it. Times have changed and so has the formulation for many laundry detergents. Some powdered laundry detergents now contain sawdust, which is used as a filler.

Dirty Words

Beware of towels made in China and Taiwan that claim they are 100 percent cotton. These towels are not tested or regulated by the government and usually contain 20 percent polyester. These towels are not known as microfiber. Microfiber contains 60 to 85 percent polyester. These are mostly cotton but contain some polyester but not enough to be classified microfiber.

The sawdust left in your car wash towels after they have been laundered could be scratching your car. Also if you don't get all the detergent rinsed out, the towel will leave streaks on the surface of your vehicle. Switch to an organic soap and never use fabric softeners or dryer sheets. Come clean with your towels by pouring ½ cup of white vinegar in the fabric softener dispenser. It removes the detergent to prevent streaks and scratches.

Drying

Some folks allow their cars to drip dry after washing and wonder why they see spots before their eyes. Always dry your vehicle to prevent

water spots. Silicone-blade car squeegees (find them in automotive supply stores) do a fast job pulling water from the surface of a vehicle, boat,
or plane. Finish with a terry towel.

Never use a microfiber towel to dry a vehicle unless you intend to
repaint it. Microfiber will eventually scratch the finish off the body of
the vehicle. People love a leather chamois, but be aware that they can
strip the wax off the surface. The fake chamois are 100 percent polyester, or the same material as microfiber.

Wax On, Wax Off

The example of "wax on, wax off" from the *Karate Kid* movie has been
used a time or two in this book. It's a great example of how to clean
inside your home using both hands, but stop there. Leave the *Karate Kid*
in the ring when it comes to waxing a vehicle, including boats and RVs.

You know not to sand wood across the grain. Why? Right—it scratches
the wood. Vehicles are painted with a left-to-right and right-to-left
motion. Paint is not applied in circles. Wipe with the grain of the
paint—never against it. Now let's take a look at this confusing world of
waxes and polishes.

Knowledge Rules!

When a child is young and you give her a new food to eat, she sometimes gives the food back to you in one form or another. She is clearly
stating that this food is not going in her mouth.

When it comes to car waxes, children know best. Car waxes do not
always list what is in the product. Some companies try to be evasive by
saying the contents are "proprietary" information so it sounds formi-
dable enough to con you into a sale. If you run across a product that
sounds intriguing but the contents are not disclosed, be like a young
child and shove it back on the shelf.

It is your vehicle. You are the one who has to pay for a new paint job if
the car product damages the sealant or paint, and some of them do just
that. If the car product is safe to use, the manufacturer should proudly
list the contents. Don't take a chance—knowledge rules!

When, What, and Where of Waxes

Various chemicals are used to make up car "waxes." The job of a wax or protectant is to protect paint from oxidation caused by the UV sun rays. Choosing the wrong car care product might lead to disaster. Here is a list of the most common products used in waxes or protectants and why to avoid some of them:

- **Carnauba wax.** Technically, when the word *wax* is used to describe a car care product, it means that product contains carnauba. Because carnauba wax is solid, it needs another chemical, usually a petroleum distillate, to keep it in a liquid state.

  Carnauba wax protects against UV ray damage, but it penetrates through the paint and seals the body. This is fine if the body is metal. However, if the body is fiberglass, it could mean disaster. Fiberglass must breathe to stay "healthy." Once sealed by carnauba wax, it can turn yellow. Look at white boats in a marina or RVs in an RV park; some will have a yellow tinge. That is the yellowing caused by carnauba wax.

- **Polymers.** Referred to as protectants because they do not contain wax yet they protect against UV ray damage the same as wax. Polymers do not penetrate paint like carnauba and are recommended for all body structures. A polymer stays on the vehicle surface, and unlike carnauba wax, makes the surface slick. Bugs wipe right off and rain sheets down from the sides so the vehicle doesn't accumulate as much dirt.

- **Petroleum distillates.** These have two jobs in a car care product. First, they keep carnauba wax in a liquid state. Second, they keep chemicals mixed together.

  Some paint companies advise against using car products containing distillates. Distillates can deteriorate a clear coat or gel coat finish resulting in oxidized paint. 3M and Avery, who make the material used for decals, lettering, and stripes, specifically state not to use distillates because they dissolve the adhesive that binds the stripping to the side.

  How do you know if a product contains distillates? That is the tricky part because a wax or protectant can contain small amounts of distillate and not state so on the bottle. Look for products that specify "No Distillates" on the bottle, or request the Material Safety Data Sheet (MSDS). On the MSDS sheet look for the words *aliphatic hydrocarbon*, *mineral oil*, *petroleum*, or *hydrocarbon*. Those are a few of the alternative names for distillates.

♦ **Silicone.** This is another tricky additive to car products. If a car product does not list the ingredients, it's usually made with silicone. Companies never want to tell you their product contains silicone because of the dangers associated with using it. If a company says its product ingredients are "proprietary information," it could be a signal that the product contains silicone.

Like distillates, silicone can deteriorate paint. The problem with silicone comes into play if your vehicle is already starting to oxidize when you apply the silicone, or if the silicone deteriorates the paint and it begins to oxidize. Most body shops won't paint a vehicle after silicone has been applied. It's difficult to completely remove silicone, so a bit is left on the vehicle. If you have ever tried to paint over silicone window caulking, you know paint doesn't stick to it.

New car paint won't stick to the residual silicone left on the body of the vehicle. It ends up looking like "fish eyes," and three months later the paint bubbles and peels off the sides.

> **Dirty Words**
>
> Beware of products that tell you to add a capful to a bucket of water. It is supposed to wash and shine the vehicle. They are usually silicone unless the bottle states otherwise.

♦ **Teflon.** The research Mary has done on Teflon has come up empty-handed for problems. Some companies apply a Teflon coating to a vehicle. Although expensive, it does seem to work.

Choosing a Wax

Hands down, a polymer-based protectant will give you excellent protection from damage caused by the elements. Look for one that does not contain petroleum distillates.

Dirty Words

Many of the car waxes or protectants are called "waterless washes and protectants." That means they clean a vehicle without water. The product is designed to emulsify or dissolve dirt. However, no product can emulsify sand. Do not use these products if your car is gritty. The sand will scratch the paint.

It is just as important that your protectant contain kaolin clay. If you run your hand across the surface of a vehicle, you will feel little bumps in the paint called *impurities*. Unless the impurities are removed, they can damage the paint by allowing water to settle into the tiny pin drop-sized holes. The kaolin clay contained in a good protectant not only removes those impurities, but also seals the tiny hole left behind.

How Often Is Often Enough?

How often should you use a protectant on your vehicle? That depends on your circumstances. Any vehicle—whether it's a boat, an RV, or a car—that is outside in the elements during the majority of the day should be treated with a protectant four times the first year, three times the following year, and then twice a year after that. After a year of applying your protectant, you start building layers of protection that last a long time.

If your vehicle is parked under cover half the year, apply a protectant twice a year. Apply another coat if the rain is no longer sheeting down; or if the vehicle begins to look dull.

Always apply protectant to the roof and hood three to four times a year. The sun beats down on those surfaces all day and quickly deteriorates the paint. Likewise, salt, sand, snow, and ice during the winter can cause damage so winterize your vehicle at the beginning of the season and apply two coats to the bottom where salt and sand hit hardest.

First, if paint is coming off your vehicle when you wash or apply a protectant and you are applying it once or twice a year, you need to bump that up to three to four times. The sun is deteriorating your gel or clear coat finish, and it needs help. If you are oxidizing, you actually need a sealant to remove it.

Mary's Handy Hints _____

To remove oxidation or the whitish look from lettering, decals, or striping on a vehicle, boat, airplane, motorcycle, truck, trailer, or van, spray it with a foaming tub and tile cleaner. It removes the oxidation and brings back the color. That stuff is very toxic so never use it inside your home. Wear gloves.

Second, if you are protecting your vehicle two to three times a year and you are oxidizing, it means your protectant either contains silicone or a low-grade petroleum distillate. A low-grade distillate will "eat" through the finish and cause the paint to deteriorate. If this is the case, use a sealant or oxidation remover to get rid of the oxidation. Maguire's, 303, and Mary Moppins all have excellent oxidation removers. Wait for 24 hours; then apply a high-grade protectant and again three times within the next year to stop any further oxidation.

The Inside View

If the interior of your car could talk, it would beg for more attention than just a quick vacuum of the carpet. Vacuuming is a good start. Now let's complete the job and even find a few ways to prevent a potentially disastrous spill.

Use additional floor mats to protect the carpet—a must if you have young children or pets. The additional mat protects your original carpet and mat from major spills or pet accidents.

Next, purchase a white plastic table cloth to put down on the back seat if you do have children or pets. Turn the fuzzy side upward and place a light-colored, body-size bath towel or beach towel on top of that. The towel catches the spills while the plastic protects the seats. Personally, I'd rather machine wash a towel than scrub seat cushions.

Wipe down the face of the dash and windows with your organic glass cleaner. The off-gassing from vinyl creates a film that distorts your vision and makes driving hazardous. That "new car" smell is the off-gassing from vinyl as well as flame and stain retardants in carpet and upholstery. These products cause serious health issues discussed earlier. Keep a window cracked open for two years after buying a new vehicle.

Clean leather or vinyl with a cleaner specially made for leather and vinyl. It prevents oil and dirt from gaining ground in those surfaces. A good conditioner prevents drying and cracking. Some leather care products are both a cleaner and conditioner.

Your organic cleaner or a pine essential oil diluted in carrier oil does a good job removing most stains from carpet and cloth seats. Nature's Miracle works wonders for pet accidents and spilled milk from sippy cups or baby bottles.

For the sake of your health, when you purchase a new vehicle ask for fabric seats that contain no stain or fire retardants. If the car cannot be ordered without those additives, consider a used vehicle so all the toxic fumes have off-gassed. The added benefit of purchasing a used vehicle is the energy and natural resources saved in the manufacturing process of a new vehicle.

The Least You Need to Know

- ◆ Father may not know best when it comes to cleaning a vehicle.

- ◆ A little vinegar and water, properly washed towels, and the right equipment give you a good start when it comes to washing your car.

- ◆ Do your research before choosing a product to protect your vehicle.

- ◆ Be fussy when it comes to keeping the interior of your vehicle clean.

Part 4

That's Not All, Folks:
Other Cleaning Challenges

If you have ever been hampered by laundry, driven to extremes cleaning your car, ridden through the mud on your bike, or gone batty cleaning the furnace ducts then this section is your basic boot camp to cleaning all the odds and ends including Fido. You'll receive a bird's-eye view on Mary's new Precision Cleaning Methods. Mary just sent spced cleaning packing back into the dark ages.

Chapter 14

Laundry Room Bliss

In This Chapter

- ◆ Whitening whites and brightening brights
- ◆ Deciphering laundry cycles
- ◆ Conserving energy while laundering is easier than you think
- ◆ Don't forget to clean your dryer

It piles up on the floor and threatens to take over the bathroom. If your teenage son is anything like mine was growing up, the smell could make a skunk seem pleasant.

I'm talking dirty laundry folks and not the kind where you confess all your sins to the world. Okay, for you younger folks, there was a saying back in the '50s: "He aired his dirty laundry to the world." It meant some public figure confessed to a grievous sin. In fact, back in days of yore Monday was the traditional laundry day. It was such an onerous task to drag out the washboard or wringer washer, that the day was labeled "Blue Monday."

Let's air our own "dirty laundry" and fess up to not knowing whether to wash light-colored clothes with the whites or colors and the right water temperature to use.

Prep Clothes Before They Hit the Hamper

Face it, we've all hurriedly grabbed an armful of clothes not caring about their color or weight and tossed them into the washer hoping the machine was forgiving enough to clean them. The toss-and-go method works if you don't mind reddish spots on your favorite white shirt or towel lint on your pants.

Gather your dirty clothes and sort them following these guidelines:

1. **Washing method.** People often advise sorting clothes according to different fabric weights and types of clothing. This works fine if you have more than two people in your family and run five or six loads of laundry at one time. Be considerate to Mother Earth. Running several small, separate loads of laundry consumes excessive water and energy, and it adds an extra burden on the budget.

   Begin by sorting heavier white and light-colored clothing, like sweats and pants, in one pile. Lighter-weight whites and light-colored clothing like undergarments and shirts go into a second pile. Do the same for dark clothes. Heavyweight dark clothes include jeans and sweatshirts. If there is not enough laundry to fill the washing machine for all four piles, combine the light-colored clothes into one pile and the dark-colored clothes into a second pile. Mary has been combining weights of clothing since she left home 30 years ago without a hitch.

   As you sort your clothes, set aside any clothes that need to be hand washed or be washed on the gentle cycle. If you have but a few of these items, wash them by hand to save the energy of machine washing.

Mary's Handy Hints _____

A fast alternative to hand washing is to order a Handwasher from Lehman's Mail Order Catalog. It is a miniature washing machine that sets on a counter. Your arm supplies the two minutes of energy it takes to clean clothes, which is faster than washing clothes in the sink. Call 330-857-1111 or go to www.lehmans.com.

2. **Color.** The basic groupings are white, medium, and dark. Here are the specifics:

    White. White (of course), pale yellow, beige, light blue, light gray, and misty green.

    Medium. Depending on the number of clothes you are laundering, wash medium-colored clothes with the light colors, except for darker pinks. Medium colors include sky blue, mint green, tan, gray, yellow, khaki, and camel.

    Mary's Handy Hints

    Anything with red shading should be washed together, including red, dark pink, and purple. New blue jeans should be laundered with other blue jeans the first few times.

    Dark. Navy blue, brown, blue jeans, green, dark green, and charcoal grey. Some pinks can be washed with dark colors—test for color fastness first.

3. **Amount or type of soil.** As you sort, put heavily soiled clothing into a pile all its own. You don't want grease ending up on your good blouse. After washing greasy items, be sure to wipe down the washer and dryer tubs with your concentrated all-purpose cleaner and rinse. Grease and oil can stick to the tubs and contaminate your next load of clothes.

Deciphering Cleaning Labels

The time to read the cleaning label on clothing is before you bring it home, especially if the clothing is dry clean only. See "Dry-Cleaning Cautions" at the end of the chapter for warnings.

Many pieces of clothing that say "dry clean only" can be laundered by hand. Silk is one of those fabrics, as are wool and cashmere. Silk will not shrink and does quite well being hand washed in cool water using an organic detergent like Bi-O-Kleen or an organic liquid hair shampoo like Aubrey.

Mary was told by the director of the Western Wool Yarn Association that Woolite has changed its formula and is no longer safe to use on wool yarn or fabric. They recommend Brown Sheep Shampoo. (www. brownsheep.com or 1-800-826-9136).

Dirty Words

If you turn your clothes inside out before you launder them, your T-shirts won't pile, pants and jeans don't wear so quickly, and good blouses and shirts will keep their color longer. Pretreat any soiled spots with your organic cleaner before laundering.

Always test a small, unnoticeable spot first to determine whether the fabric can be hand washed. If a label says to wash the clothing in warm water, you can wash it in cold. Just don't wash it in hot water unless you are on a diet and going to lose a full clothing size by the end of the wash cycle. It will either shrink or turn from red to pink. If the directions specify "wash in cold water," it's not okay to use warm water.

Launder with Our Earth in Mind

The Department of Energy reports that nearly 90 percent of the energy consumed for washing clothes comes from heating the water. Why is hot water needed to clean clothing? Most laundry detergent manufacturers specify using hot water to kill the germs and to get clothes clean.

Let's back up for a second and look at that last sentence. Hot water needed to get the clothes clean and kill germs? First of all, most germs survive a very short period of time on any surface. A germ that is going to invade your body from clothing will do so while you are wearing the garment. It will not live long enough to contaminate you after it sits three or four days in the hamper and then goes through the wash cycle *and* dryer heat.

The next recommendation by laundry detergent companies calls for hot water to dissolve the detergent and clean your clothes. Maybe my thinking is all turned around, but I thought the purpose of a laundry detergent was to dissolve in water so it could clean the clothes. If hot water is necessary to get clothes clean, doesn't that mean your detergent isn't working?

Test your powdered detergent by pouring a teaspoon in a glass jar and fill it with a cup of cold water. Stir until it dissolves. The next day, if you see a slimy film or more than a bit of residue at the bottom, the detergent probably is made from sawdust or filler. Even in cold water, an organic detergent (most do not contain fillers) will stay nearly 95 percent dissolved.

Reduce the amount of energy you consume by using cool to warm water. Use the permanent press setting rather than the regular cycle to save further energy. Plus, the permanent press cycle is less abrasive on clothing so your clothes last longer.

Here is another way to save your health and our Mother Earth:

Stop using dryer sheets and expensive fabric softeners. Add ½ cup—more if needed—of vegetable- or grain-based distilled white vinegar to the rinse cycle for top-loading machines and ⅓ cup for front-loading machines. It pulls the detergent out of clothing so your skin won't itch, and it is a proven disinfectant, and softens clothes.

 Mary's Handy Hints

When you need to replace your washer, invest in a front-loading washing machine. They use less water, do a better job cleaning clothes, and put less stress on clothes so they last longer.

Finally, for best washing results in top-loading machines, begin filling your machine by adding ½ cup distilled vinegar and your detergent. Pour another ½ cup of vinegar into the fabric softener cup. Swish the detergent until it is dissolved—about 30 seconds—then add your clothes. Clothes cannot come clean unless the detergent is completely dissolved.

Here's how you can break down cold, warm, and hot water for laundering:

♦ **Cold water is 80°F (26.7°C) or colder.** Use cold water for delicate items, clothing that is lightly soiled, permanent press, protein stains such as blood, garments with dyes that may bleed or run, and the final rinse of the wash cycle.

♦ **Warm water is from 90°F to 100°F (32.2°C–43.3°C).** Use warm for color fast brights and dark colors.

◆ **Hot water is 130°F (54.4°C) or above.** You only need hot water for heavily soiled or greasy rags or clothing. It may also be preferable for towels and diapers.

Use an organic detergent such as Bi-O-Kleen or The Clean Team's Red Juice, and you rarely need hot water. Bi-O-Kleen is gentle enough for delicates so you don't need Woolite-type detergents.

The Regular Cycle

Sturdy cottons, towels, and heavily soiled clothes should be washed in the regular cycle. Presoak heavily soiled clothing.

The Permanent Press Cycle

Wash cotton, bedding, undergarments, and synthetic fibers other than acrylic, modacrylic, acetate, and rayon (which require hand washing or the gentle cycle) on the permanent press cycle. Shorter than the regular cycle, the permanent press cycle provides a cool-down rinse and a cold final rinse plus a slower spin speed to prevent wrinkles from setting into synthetic fabrics.

The Gentle or Delicate Cycle

Use the gentle or delicate cycle for washable lace, lingerie, nylons, and other clothing that indicates gentle treatment on the care label. This cycle has a short, slow agitation cycle, cool to warm water, and a cold rinse. Use a mild detergent for this cycle. Preferably use the Hand-washer from Lehman's.

Dirty Words ─────────────────────────

Never use hydrogen peroxide or bleach on silk, wool, or dry-clean-only clothing. Do not use chlorine bleach, especially on baby clothing. Your skin—especially that of babies and young children— absorb the toxin from the bleach. Switch to hydrogen peroxide or borax.

A Look at Healthy Helpful Washing Options

Do your white clothes appear dingy even though you bleach them?
Toss the bottle of bleach. It causes not only skin irritations, but also a
host of other serious medical problems. Add ½ cup of 35 percent food-
grade hydrogen peroxide or powdered laundry whitener per regular
washer. To remove the dingy gray caused by bleach, allow the clothes
to soak in the washer for 30 minutes after adding the peroxide and
detergent. Then wash normally. White and colored clothes perk
right up.

Dryer Rules

Now that your clothes are clean, you need to dry them using the least
possible amount of energy. What should and *shouldn't* go into the
dryer? Most machine washable items can be dried in the dryer. There
are exceptions, naturally:

- ◆ Rubber, plastics (including microfiber), and fiberglass

- ◆ Acetate, acrylic, spandex, and delicates like viscose rayon

- ◆ Drip-dry clothing and flannel. Flannel sheets can be machine dried

- ◆ Wools other than Superwash
  and other treated wools

Mary's Handy Hints

Fill your dryer only half
full. Overfilling can lead
to wrinkled clothing that
takes hours to dry.

Follow these directions for dryer
settings to prevent clothing
shrinking to the size of a Barbie
doll's:

- ◆ Regular is the hottest temperature setting. Use it for sturdy cottons such as towels and preshrunk jeans.

- ◆ Use the Medium setting to dry permanent press clothing, synthetics, some knits, and lightweight cottons and linens.

- ◆ Save the Low or Delicate setting for cotton knits, lingerie, and
  sheer fabrics.

Follow the instructions on the care label. The label will tell you
whether the garment can be dried and at which temperature setting.

> **Dirty Words**
>
> Never leave home with the dryer running. If you must leave, turn off the dryer until you return. Dryers are a leading cause of house fires. If you aren't home, it can save you from losing everything. Be safe out there. Turn off the dryer.

Clean the Filter

More than 15,000 homes a year catch on fire because of lint left in the dryer vents. Clean the filter after every load of clothing. Then once a week remove the filter and whisk around the area just under the filter with a lambswool duster.

Don't stop with the filter. Twice a year when you change the batteries in your smoke detectors, let that remind you to clean the vent located at the rear of your dryer. Clean the piping as well. Remove the piping and run your lambswool duster through the piping, or use the brush attachment to your vacuum cleaner.

Save on Energy

Most heavy clothing like sweatshirts and blue jeans need only be dried for 15–20 minutes to remove the wrinkles. Hang them to finish drying and reduce the amount of energy you use by 60 percent. You will often find it necessary to dry heavier-weight clothes with lightweight items like white cotton tube socks and light-colored shirts.

The drying time could take 50 minutes for the socks to dry. Set your timer for 30 minutes; then remove the lightweight clothes, which are dry. With fewer clothes in the dryer, heavier items finish drying in 10 minutes, saving 10 minutes of energy.

Ten minutes energy on 1 load of clothes weekly equals 520 minutes of saved energy each year. Multiply that by the 70 million households in the United States, and it comes to a mere 36 billion 400 million minutes of saved energy.

Looking for a place to hang wet clothes to dry? Invest in a tension rod that extends from wall to wall in your shower or tub enclosure. Put it up high to prevent it from being in the way of taking a shower. Hang your clothes on the rod to dry.

Dry-Cleaning Cautions

Dry cleaning is expensive and the solvent used—tetrachloroethylene, otherwise known as perchloroethylene (PERC)—is carcinogenic over long-term, low-level exposure. It can cause kidney and liver damage, neurological impairment, and vision problems. It has been associated with reproduction disorders as well as developmental problems in unborn children, babies, and young children. As a chlorinated compound, it is a precursor of dioxin.

People are moving away from dry cleaning for that reason. Never bring dry cleaning directly into your home. Always leave the clothing in the garage for several days. Dioxin bioaccumulates in your body. It never goes away and can be deadly.

The Least You Need to Know

◆ Sorting clothes properly is the key to proper cleaning.

◆ Some clothing care labels can be ignored.

◆ Match up your wash cycle, water temperature, and detergent for the best results.

◆ Be energy efficient when it comes to washing and drying your clothes.

Chapter 15

Loose Ends

In This Chapter

- ◆ Critter comforts
- ◆ Taking care of sporting equipment
- ◆ TLC for stuffed animals and toys
- ◆ Cleaning kid's stuff: High chairs, strollers, and car seats

Loose ends—we tie 'em up, sort 'em out, piece 'em together, pull 'em tight, hang onto 'em, and when nothing else works we sift through loose ends keeping the ones we need and tossing the rest. And all that said in one breath!

It may take you more than a breath or two to clean up, shape up, and condition your assortment of bikes, car seats, bowling balls, baseball gloves, stuffed animals, dogs, cats, or fish. In this chapter, these loose ends are pulled together to give you Earth- and human-friendly solutions to keep them clean.

Cleaning Your Critter's Area

Back in 1990, a group called Pet Shop Boys released an album called *Behaviour*, which contained the song "Jealousy." In the song, they sum up the world of pets as pets display a variety of "behaviors" from "jealousy" to excitement.

Along with these behaviors comes a range of other issues like smelly kitty litter, fleas, and the floor being used as a potty. Let's solve those issues without toxic chemicals or sprays.

TLC for Dogs and Cats

These loveable four-leggeds are known to be man's and woman's best friend, until they display one of those behavioral issues and urinate or defecate on the carpet.

Wet or dry vacs quickly absorb large amounts of liquids. Then you can use several towels to finish the job. Walk on the towel with your shoes on to help absorb the moisture. Heat sets a stain so resist the temptation to use a steam cleaner.

Enzyme products such as Kleen-Free (www.kleen-free.com), Nature's Miracle (found at pet stores), or PetGuest (www.petguest.com) do a superb job destroying stains and odors. Enzymes eat away at bacteria and solid waste matter. They are unmatched in their ability to destroy urine, feces, vomit odors, and stains.

Mary's Handy Hints

When I researched enzyme products for cleaning pet stains and odors, I was impressed with Kleen-Free. According to their information, it takes care of stains and odors; kills fleas, lice, and bedbugs; and treats pests on plants and garden crops.

Read Appendix B, including the introduction, for complete instructions on removing urine and fecal matter from carpet, furniture, and bedding.

Fleas: Dogs and cats must be combed regularly with a flea comb to remove fleas and their larvae. Vacuum all floor surfaces daily for 10 days to remove fleas and immerging larvae. Remove the vacuum bag everyday and seal it in a plastic bag to prevent reinfestation in your home. Set the bag in the sun or in your freezer, if you have room, to kill the fleas.

After vacuuming the first day, spray the carpet with a nontoxic flea killer like Kleen-Free, or look for a natural one at pet stores. Damp-mop your hard floor surfaces using a vinegar and water solution—do not use this on stone floors.

Use dry borax sprinkled on stone or wood floors if you see fleas after vacuuming. Let the borax set on the floor for five or six hours, keeping pets and children off those surfaces until after you have vacuumed again.

Add a couple ounces of 100 percent pure castile oil soap, which contains peppermint, coconut, and jojoba oils, to the Kleen-Free to treat your yard. Castile soap also repels ticks.

Brewer's yeast added to your pet's food repels fleas as does adding a teaspoon of apple cider to their drinking water. Finally, toss cedar chips into their bedding.

Bath time: Take care with the shampoo you use to bathe your pet. The toxins in that shampoo penetrate their skin as well as yours. Pets don't like perfumed scents, so buy unscented soap.

 Mary's Handy Hints

Keep fleas, ticks, and mosquitoes off any pets, kids, and you by checking out "The Bug Band." www.bughand.net. I attached them to my dog's collar and he never had a flea. They are made from geranium oil and are 100 percent nontoxic.

A few drops of castile soap (mentioned previously) added to an enzyme product like Kleen-Free cleans your pet and kills fleas and ticks. Give them a final rinse with one part white vinegar to four parts water to restore their natural skin tone.

Frequent bathing dries their skin, so bathe pets once a month.

Pet hair: When you have a pet you have hair. You can spend an hour cleaning the hair off your furniture and floors, or you can take 10 minutes once a day to brush your pet. Worth the effort? You bet! Use a flea comb on their neck to check for fleas.

Washing pet bowls: Clean pet bowls in the bathtub. After washing, wipe with straight vinegar. The slobber in their bowls does not belong in the sink where you prepare dinner. If you wash their bowls in the kitchen sink, clean it with hot soapy water and then wipe it with straight vinegar.

Kitty litter: You'll find a host of various kitty litters on the market. Testing them is the only way to find which works best for your furry friend. Clean them with Bi-O-Kleen, CleanEz, or castile soap and hot water once a week. Then wipe them with vinegar or an enzyme product to kill the odor and bacteria.

Hair balls: Now there is a not-so-pleasant treat for you. Add $\frac{1}{2}$ teaspoon of corn oil or safflower oil to your cats' food twice a month. The oil coats their intestines so hair slides on down rather than gathering into balls. Vary the amount until you find what works best for your cat.

Other Four-Legged Creatures

It just doesn't seem like childhood unless a child has a pet turtle, mouse, gerbil, hamster, or rabbit in his room. Your *child* is cleaning the cage, right?

Turtles: Because turtles are messy little critters when they eat, feed them in a separate tank. Then their main tank can be cleaned every 45 days rather than weekly. They urinate and defecate in the tank, so clean the residue daily for a healthy turtle.

Scrub the tank with baking soda and a white scrub pad dampened with straight vinegar. Then rinse the tank with straight vinegar and finish by rinsing the tank three or four times with water. Clean "decorations" with a toothbrush and baking soda.

Mice, gerbils, and hamsters: I bet your child didn't count on cleaning the cage weekly, but weekly it must be done or the smell will become overpowering. Animals are sensitive to smells, so use an enzyme cleaner for the cage. Enzyme cleaners kill bacteria but don't upset the pet. Dry the cage before putting in new bedding.

Rabbits: Should they get loose in the house, they will gnaw on furniture. So "rabbit-proof" your home. Change their water and clean their cage daily with an enzyme cleaner because rabbits are sensitive critters.

Dirty Words ————————————————————

Think twice before buying a rabbit for your child. They bite and scratch humans and need daily attention and exercise because their bones break easily. Children tend to be rough on animals. Perhaps a hamster would be a better choice.

Clean Tanks = Healthy Fish

It is not within the scope of this book to cover cleaning all the varieties of fish tanks. Let's take a look at the most common tank, which is a community tank or one in which two to three types of fish "commune" peacefully together.

Do your research before buying supplies and fish. Have the tank set up and ready to receive your fish when you bring them home. Part of those supplies should be tongs for grabbing things off the bottom of the tank, and of course a fish net.

Clean the tank every two to three weeks; otherwise, it will turn into an all-day chore. Scrub the tank thoroughly with a white scrub pad and an enzyme cleaner. If the tank is green or moldy, clean it with straight vinegar and then straight hydrogen peroxide. Let each set for several minutes; then clean with the enzyme cleaner. Rinse the tank several times before refilling with water.

Check the pumps and heater to make sure they are working properly. Clean all the tank decorations with a toothbrush each time you clean the tank. Fish depend on a clean environment and properly working equipment to stay healthy and alive.

Birds of a Feather

Whether you have a parrot or other kind of bird, her cage must be kept clean on a daily basis; otherwise, your bird could become ill. Pull the water and food containers every day and clean them with an organic liquid dish soap. Rinse the containers thoroughly and dry them completely before refilling them. Change the liner every day. If your bird is a tidy bird, then every other day will do just fine. After pulling the lining, dampen a cloth with an enzyme cleaner listed previously and wipe all the surfaces. Use a bird-safe cage cleaner to remove the tough stuff.

Sporting Equipment

Ah, you just returned from a wonderful 25-mile bike ride through the country and you want to rest on the back patio with a cool glass of lemonade. Only along comes this lady out of some cleaning book saying you need to clean your bike. Is she out of her right mind? Well, as a matter of fact, I lost my right mind a long time ago and my left mind was never worth a hoot in the first place. Yes, clean your bike, along with your baseball glove, and golf clubs (if you like improved scores)—and it doesn't hurt to brush off that basketball once in awhile either.

Keeping your gear in gear means it will last longer. It also prevents mold—something you folks in dry, hot states like Arizona know little about—and it reduces infections.

Serious infections, though, crop up with the sharing of equipment like football uniforms, judo mats, and even basketballs. Let's take a closer look into this nasty world of germs.

Boot Camp and MRSA

So you send your child off to school where he wants to play a sport. In school situations, helmets and uniforms are usually passed from student to student. Cuts happen and then sweat soaks the clothing and helmets with possible germs from the bleeding cuts.

Methicilin-resistant staphylococcus aureus (MRSA) is a nasty little virus that is resistant to many antibiotics. Often contracted in hospitals, it can be passed on through shared sports equipment, including helmets, padding, and mats. Then it is called community-associated MRSA. It is passed through skin-to-skin contact or when an open sore comes into contact with a wrestling, judo, or gymnastics mat or things like baseball helmets.

The National Institute of Health and Safety suggests practicing good hygiene by doing the following:

◆ Keep cuts and scrapes clean and covered with a bandage.

◆ Avoid contact with other people's wounds or bandages.

◆ Do not share personal items such as toweling or clothes.

◆ Wash soiled sheets, towels, and clothes that come in contact with a cut in hot water with bleach. Dry them in a hot dryer.

◆ See a health-care provider if the wound becomes infected. The infection must be treated with antibiotics; otherwise, serious illness can occur, not only for the person but others as well.

Check with your child's coach, instructor, or school to ensure the lockers, mats, helmets, padding, and so on are disinfected and cleaned regularly.

Dirty Words

Fitness centers are social places where MRSA can be spread. Take your own bottle of antiseptic spray to wipe off the machines. Yes, the spas provide bottles, but they are touched by dozens of people who might have hand infections or other skin problems.

Bicycles

Clean your helmet frequently with mild soap like castile soap to remove sweat. Bacteria can build up and cause itchy scalp. Always clean your helmet if you loan it to someone. It takes but a few minutes to wipe down the inside with an enzyme cleaner after each ride. Wash it regularly, following the helmet directions. Helmet material varies and so does cleaning them.

Cleaning your bicycle is beyond the scope of this book because it entails chains, brakes, and gears. Do an online search for the manufacturer of your bike and follow those directions.

Mary's Handy Hints

Here are a few websites to give you the basics on cleaning your bike: www.trinewbies.com/BikeClean/Welcome.asp, www.bikeexchange.com.au/article/bike-cleaning, www.mtbonline.co.za/info/bike-chain-cleaning.htm (check this one out to learn the best way to clean mountain bike chains).

Hole in One

So the chip off the old block isn't chipping so hot anymore? When was the last time your clubs received a bit of TLC? You chew them out when "they" send the ball into the sand trap, but how often do you clean them?

Never use hot water, liquid dish soap, or a degreaser on clubs. They all loosen the ferrule. Begin filling a bucket with cool to lukewarm water and a bit of organic laundry detergent. Add just enough water to cover the heads of your irons. Take the bucket outside or wash them in the bathtub!

Put your clubs in the water and let them soak as you gather an old towel and a stiff-bristled toothbrush or scrub brush. Let the clubs soak a few minutes (longer if the dirt is really hardened); then clean in the direction of the grooves with the toothbrush. Rinse (do not allow water to run up into the shaft) and dry the head and the shaft thoroughly.

Never soak woods in water. Use a cloth dampened in the sudsy water to wipe them clean and the toothbrush to clean the grooves. Wipe with a clean cloth and dry. Always keep a towel attached to your bag to clean as you swing.

See the next section to clean and condition your bag.

Things Made with Leather

Bicycle seats, sports bags, and athletic shoes have one thing in common: they need attention, too. Anything made of leather or vinyl must be cleaned and conditioned to prevent drying and cracking, especially sporting equipment due to the intense moisture and temperature changes it endures.

To take the P.U. out of tennis shoes spray an enzyme product like Nature's Miracle or Kleen-Free inside the shoes. Enzymes attack the bacteria that send out those not-so-friendly smells. Don't forget to spray the inside of gym bags or bike seats if they get a little pungent.

Cleaning and conditioning leather and vinyl involves the same process whether you are working on a bag, shoes, or a bicycle seat. Foaming shaving cream does a fair job removing some stains, such as grass, grease, and heavy soil. Never use a degreasing cleaner on leather or vinyl. Use only products specifically made for leather. Remember that "cheap ain't good and good ain't cheap," which really applies to leather and vinyl treatments. The cheap stuff will cost you hundreds of dollars replacing bags, shoes, seats, and so on.

You can find excellent leather and vinyl cleaners and conditioners on the market. Make certain the product you choose is free of chemicals, including petroleum distillates and silicone. Use a beeswax-based product for conditioning and water repellency. Mary Moppins carries Leather/Vinyl Care; another excellent product is made by Oakwood from Australia (www.oakwoodusa.net).

Stuffed Animals and Plastic Toys

When buying stuffed animals or plastic toys, make sure they are washable. After all, toys end up in the child's mouth, in the dog's mouth, and on the floor at the grocery store. Before purchasing a toy, check out the safety of the toy at www.thedailygreen.com/green-homes/eco-friendly/toys. This website lists companies with age-specific, safe toys. Always research a toy manufacturer first to see whether it has had the toy tested by a third party.

Stuffed animals: Buy machine-washable stuffed animals for your child. Then wash them monthly. Vacuum stuffed animals weekly to remove dust mites and dirt. Use a soft brush to brush the hair. Never give a long-haired stuffed animal to a child still in diapers. Babies do throw up, and fecal matter tends to find its way into the toy's hair.

Plastic toys: To clean plastic toys, dampen a wash cloth and then pour on a bit of baking soda and shampoo. Clean the toy, rinse, and go. Do you like easy? I like easy. Put the toys in the tub during baby's bath time. Kids don't mind and you do double duty cleaning baby and toys together. Place plastic books in a mesh bag and launder along with towels on the gentle cycle. Plastic books can contain phthalates, though, so research before you buy them.

Mary's Handy Hints

The Consumer Product Safety Commission produces a recall letter for children's toys and furniture. Sign up at www.cpsc.gov/cpsclist.aspx.

Most stains on plastics can be removed with a paste of cream of tartar and hydrogen peroxide.

Playpens, Car Seats, High Chairs, and Strollers

Plastic high chairs, swings, strollers, and playpens can contain formaldehyde and phthalates. Thoroughly research any brand before you buy. Use cotton bedding and solid wood furniture. Used furniture is best because it has already off-gassed.

For more information on children's furniture, read the articles on www.asehaqld.org.au and www.checnet.org.

Dirty Words

For the safety of you and your child, research before you purchase furniture for baby or you. Think twice about replacing furniture, carpeting, or hard surface flooring during your pregnancy and until the child is eight or nine years of age. See Chapter 2 for toxins in these furnishings.

Because your baby or young child probably chews and sucks on the plastic parts of these products, never clean them with a regular cleaner. Organic or not, that cleaner does not belong in your child's mouth.

These basic instructions apply to car seats, strollers, playpens, and high chairs. First, take the piece to the backyard or lay plastic down on the garage floor. Disassemble the piece by laying it out flat for cleaning.

Mix one cup distilled white vinegar to four cups water, adding a teaspoon of baking soda. Pour on a cloth and wipe the surface. If your child has been ill, wipe down the surfaces with Nature's Miracle or another enzyme product before you clean it to kill any germs.

To clean into the little nooks and crannies of these products, purchase a foam paintbrush at the hardware store. Dampen the brush in the vinegar solution to clean those tight areas.

Straps on children's furniture are notorious for being covered with gooey food and other surprises Mom and Dad may not even be aware

are there. It is important to keep the straps clean. Because children rarely put them in their mouths, they can safely be cleaned by soaking them first with sudsy water, letting that set for 20–30 minutes, and then scrubbing with a damp cloth.

Place an old cotton tube sock on one hand, like you do for dusting, and dampen it with the vinegar solution. It does a quick job wiping down these surfaces on a daily basis. You can even pick up food crumbs with the socked hand!

The Least You Need to Know

◆ Ignorance is not bliss when it comes to keeping your loose ends clean and tidy.

◆ Wait until your child has proven she can handle chores without fussing before allowing her to have a pet.

◆ Always carry a bottle of an enzyme product or hand sanitizer when you play sports to treat shared equipment.

◆ When looking for clothing, toys, or equipment for children, research before you buy.

Chapter 16

Breathe Easier by Going Green

In This Chapter

- ◆ Smokin': the furnace, fireplace, and other sources of fire
- ◆ Conditioning the air conditioner
- ◆ Understanding potential allergens and your home
- ◆ The joys of going green—houseplants, that is

You build up funds for your retirement—that's a good thing. Traffic builds up when you are running late driving to a meeting—that's not a good thing. You can build up your physical endurance—that's another good thing. Toxic fumes build up inside your home—now that is a horrible thing.

Sick home syndrome encompasses more than fumes from the chemicals you use. Dust, air fresheners, dishwasher detergent, carpeting, and more cause a list of ailments from allergies to cancer, heart problems, Attention Deficit Disorder in children, and a disruption of the central nervous system.

The good thing? You don't have to run away from home to grab a breath of fresh air. This chapter introduces you to hot spots in your home that contribute to sick home syndrome. You'll learn preventative tricks and when to call an expert for help.

Some Like It Hot: Furnaces, Fireplaces, and More

Hands down fire is the most important discovery of mankind. How else would we toast marshmallows? Cavemen wisely burned their fires outside or in well-ventilated caves.

We burn fires inside where dangerous levels of combustion can build. Fireplaces are built with chimneys to remove the by-products. Furnace exhaust pipes and vents carry their fumes outside a home. Have both professionally cleaned at the beginning of each winter.

Mary's Handy Hints _____

Change your carbon monoxide (CO) detector batteries when you change smoke alarm batteries in the fall over Labor Day weekend. Changing them on a holiday helps you remember to do it.

Smoky the Bear

Scary stuff: cigarettes emit 40 types of carcinogens. Secondhand smoke hits young children and those with lung or heart disease the hardest. The best remedy is, of course, to stop smoking. Even smoke from clothing can cause lung problems in young children. At the very least, take smoke breaks outside.

What You Don't Know, Learn

Acting like an ostrich with its head stuck in the sand does not a healthy home make. Indoor air pollution can only be solved by getting your head out of the sand and into knowledge. It means changing your ways so you live a healthy life without fear of the ailments that needlessly afflict friends and family.

Be aware of by-product emissions like carbon monoxide (CO). It is a colorless, odorless, and poisonous gas. Relatively harmless in open spaces, CO can be deadly if allowed to accumulate, such as when running gas-powered machinery in your garage. In fact, every year more people die of CO poisoning than from any other type of poisoning.

Protect yourself and your family from this invisible menace with a CO detector. The U.S. Consumer Product Safety Commission recommends placing one detector on each level of your home and in the garage. Check gas heaters for proper ventilation and leaks. Construction on many homes is so lax that gas valves might not be properly placed and can emit slow gas leakage.

Chillin' Out

Baby, it's hot outside! During the summer most areas of the country get to sizzling. Some areas suffer even more when the humidity reaches levels as high as the temperature. Along come our life saviors—the air conditioner and dehumidifier.

The filter in your air conditioner traps dust particles so they don't escape back into your home. Replace old or dirty filters with an electrostatic mesh filter, which can be bought at hardware stores. The filter is made of polypropylene plastic mesh with an electrostatic charge that attracts particles from the air. Cut it to size and clean it by mercly rinsing it out. Dry and replace.

Causes of Home Air Pollution

No one likes being trapped in a motel room with noisy neighbors. You *can* change motel rooms. By making a few changes at home, you can move unwelcomed toxic "guests" out of your home as well. Here is a brief lineup of a few toxins that invade your home.

Mary's Handy Hints

Burn 100 percent soy candles. Soy candles emit little if any smoke and do not contain lead wicks, which are toxic to breathe. Plus, they burn five times longer than regular wax candles with a gentle, non-overpowering scent.

- **Moisture.** Home and health enemies such as mold, mildew, bacteria, dust mites, dry rot, and insects thrive on moisture.

- **Cigarette smoke.** We all know the harmful effects of cigarette smoke, both first- and secondhand.

- **Combustion products.** Carbon monoxide and carbon dioxide can build up in the home from fuel-burning heating equipment, gas appliances and heaters, fireplaces, and woodstoves.

- **Particles.** Invisible to the naked eye, dust, dust mites, pollen, lead, and formaldehyde can be contaminating your home.

- **Common household chemicals.** Cleaning products emit chemical residues in your home that hang in the air for several days. Some accumulate in your body, taking a toll on your health.

- **Furniture and carpet.** Refer to Chapter 2 for the toxic problems associated with various flooring.

- **Pet hair and dander.** I love animals, but unless you keep your dog, cat, hamster, and furry critters cleaned and brushed, the sneezing is gonna getcha.

Add the fumes from paints, solvents, pesticides, and odors and you have quite the nasty trappings. Later you'll learn inexpensive, effective methods to put the boot to these pollens.

The Matter of Buildup

Okay, so you are tired of reading about buildup and the ailments that afflict you if you don't change your ways. Let me lay this one last fact on you to help you understand why I'm so adamant.

Grab a dime and place it on your forearm. That one spot of skin contains three million cells. Cells are porous so they are a two-way street for your body. They absorb things into your body from the environment and aid the liver by emitting toxins from the body.

Dirty Words

Guess what happens when you use most typical grocery store bar soaps in your shower? Right, the soap residue builds up on shower walls. Guess where else it builds up? It builds up in your cells where it blocks them from being able to excrete toxins. Soaps and hand lotions trap the toxins. Switch to a soap that is free of oil, lye, and fat. Use lotions sparingly.

The trillions of cells on your body's skin absorb everything that touches your skin, passing it along to your organs, blood, brain, and bones. No single part of your body goes unscathed by the things you eat, breathe, touch, and use. These things affect hormone balance, cell regeneration, and nerve impulses. Dementia, Parkinson's, arthritis, cancer, osteoporosis, heart and lung disease, asthma, and fibromyalgia are but a few of the problems directly related to what you use, eat, and breathe.

As I said earlier, one product used a few times won't make much of a health difference—exceptions noted. It usually takes time for problems to arise, and those problems are sneaky. They don't believe in giving you advance warnings.

Thus, you tool along in life thinking you are an exercise guru and don't need to change a thing. Whammo, the next day you have cancer and ask what went wrong. What went wrong was years of toxic buildup in your body, which is usually preventable.

Beware of Air Fresheners

Advertising does such a wonderful job laying on guilt trips. Unless we have the most recent air freshener, our home, well, stinks. There are safe ways to rid your home of smells other than air fresheners. I would rather not have reproductive and hormone disruptions that the phthalates in these fresheners cause. Phthalates are found in 85 percent of the most popular air fresheners.

It doesn't matter whether you purchase the plug-ins, sprays, plastic packages, wicks, or diffused fresheners—most contain phthalates. Even worse, they don't get rid of the smell. Most fresheners are toxic perfumes that mask odors and lead to lung problems. Many of them contain pesticides.

Dirty Words

For you diehard air freshener fans, the "natural-scented" air fresheners actually coat your nasal passage with an oil such as methoxychlor that deadens your nasal passage so you can't smell the odor. It's a pesticide that accumulates in your fat cells.

Because of its toxicity to the environment, formaldehyde has been banned from being used in holding tank products for RVs and boats, yet companies are allowed to add it to air fresheners. Talk about respiratory failure and asthma attack heaven, to say nothing of the cancer caused by formaldehyde.

The EPA in 2002 tested plug-in air fresheners. They found a list of chemicals in these products so long it would take a chemistry book to list them. A few are pinene, limonene, phenol, cresol, and aldehydes. Pinene and limonene react with ozone, which is found in every home. Combined they make formaldehyde.

Not enough to convince you to take that stuff to the toxic dump? Then try carcinogens such as acetaldehyde (or styrene), toluene, and chlorbenzene. Talk about the Great American coverup—and we aren't talking odors here, folks.

The Great Window Coverup

As long as I'm delivery a hearty blow to indoor pollutants, here is the rundown on the toxins hanging around your windows. You've already read the toxic story behind vinyl. Stay clear of plastic vinyl mini blinds. Most are made in China or Taiwan. The United States allows them to be imported with *no* testing.

U.S. Consumer Product Safety Commission tested vinyl blinds and immediately issued a warning to remove and properly dispose of these blinds. The lead found in them can be as much as 100 times the federally allowed limit.

Vinyl deteriorates, leaving a toxic lead dust on plastic blinds. Clean the blinds or wipe your finger across them and you just absorbed the lead. Think of babies and young children and how they touch things and then put their fingers in their mouths. Lead poisoning from blinds causes behavioral problems, learning disabilities, hearing problems, and growth retardation.

According to the Alliance for a Clean and Healthy Maine, manufacturers of plastics and synthetic fibers in TVs, computers, fabric furniture, curtains, and mattresses all use polybrominated diphenyl ethers (PBDEs) and brominated flame retardants (BFRs) to slow the spread of fire. A few states like Maine have banned two PBDE products: Penta and Octa.

They banned them because PBDEs are not chemically bound to plastics, which means they float from your drapes, furniture, mattresses, and carpet to other areas like your skin. When they leach out, they convert into more toxic forms like dioxin.

Don't Duck the Dirty Job of Cleaning Ducts

When home heating ducts are dirty, your system can spew dust, dirt, and mold spores into your home, increasing allergy problems. Also, dirty ducts don't work as efficiently, so heating and air-conditioning bills skyrocket.

Have your ducts cleaned professionally every two to three years—more often if you smoke, have pets, live in a dusty area, or have a family member with breathing difficulties. Remove the return register grill yearly to clean it with a lambswool duster.

Dirty Words

A word of warning: whole house purifiers can be very pricy and must be installed by a specialist. They do keep pollens out of your home and relieve the physical problems allergy sufferers face.

Pollution Solutions

Home insulations today effectively keep our houses warm in the winter and cool in the summer. However, insulation prevents your home from breathing, so pollutants have no way to escape. Old, drafty houses have an advantage after all!

As you need to replace things such as carpet, furniture, and drapes, choose natural products like real wood or stone flooring. Stay away from laminates because they contain large amounts of toxic adhesives. Wool, sisal, and jute carpeting are excellent alternatives, although wool can succumb to moth infestation so beware. Make sure fabric furniture does not contain flame retardants. Switch to real wood blinds rather than fabric drapes.

You might not be aware of the toxic buildup going on in your home because there are few clues it is happening. Here are a few inexpensive ways to keep your air clean.

Open Windows

So you want to be a shaker and mover! Well let's shake and move those toxins out of your home. I speak to thousands of people during my seminars every year. Very few are aware of sick home syndrome, let alone the fact that they can get rid of toxins just by opening windows a couple times a week. Cross ventilate by opening windows on opposite sides of the house, which pulls the breeze through your house. (Keep interior doors open!)

In a two-story home, open a downstairs window or sliding glass door and open windows upstairs to create a chimney effect that pulls air through the house.

You can increase the effectiveness by using a whole-house circulating fan such as a Patton. Set it in front of a window on, preferably, the north side or east side of the home. Cooler air that comes from the north or east is pulled into the window, while warmer air is pushed out the opposite side.

If you are allergic to tree or other outdoor pollen and opening windows worsens your symptoms, a whole-house air purifier might be your solution.

Gotta Love Those Plants

When the going gets tough and house plants jump ship, the tough get fake plants. Before you threaten to turn to fake plants because your green thumb turns brown along with the plants, keep trying. Plants solve indoor air pollution problems and help reduce if not eliminate indoor pollution.

Through photosynthesis, plants absorb pollutants and carbon dioxide through their leaves. Microbes surrounding the root system break down the contaminants and then emit pure oxygen. Just 15 houseplants in an average-size home offer a significant reduction in the number of indoor contaminants.

Mary's Handy Hints

When your plants turn brown, call your local Extension Council. Or consult master gardeners through a state college; these folks are experts at solving plant, tree, and yard problems.

Common houseplants like spider plants, philodendrons, and Boston ferns clear formaldehyde from the air. Peace lilies take care of trichloroethylene, while English ivy, chrysanthemums, and gerbera daisies have a handle on benzene. Marginata and Mother's In Law Tongue are two excellent plants for healthy indoor air.

The most useful household plants are the areca palm, golden pothos, Janet Craig, and corn plant. They do not require much light and are effective air-cleaners. Place two to three plants in a room. Wolverton's book *How to Grow Fresh Air* is a wonderful reference book on the subject of plants and indoor fresh air.

Some plants can be toxic if eaten by a child or pet so choose plants wisely.

Wonderful Vinegar and Mold

Back in the '60s and '70s we had vinyl records. When a record scratched, the needle stopped in the scratch mark playing that same section over and over. I'm much like a scratch in a vinyl record in that I repeat important issues—so repeat after me, "Prevention is the key to a clean, green home." Got that?

Good, because preventing mold is the key to improved health. If you live in a rainy or humid area, you must place dehumidifiers in your home; otherwise, mold will develop. Most important, the second you see or smell mold or mildew, you must take immediate action. One small spot today can cover the entire room by the next day.

Please, for the sake of your health, get rid of chlorine bleach. It emits dioxin, which is the most toxic chemical.

You have several natural options to get rid of mold. Mix a solution of three tablespoons of borax per cup of distilled white vinegar in a bottle. Thoroughly saturate a cloth, wiping on the mold. A one-half inch paintbrush brushes it into crevices and small areas. Leave it alone for 30 minutes; then repeat. Now wait 60 minutes and wipe to remove. If the mold is stubborn, hit it with a 50/50 solution of 35 percent food-grade peroxide to water. You don't need to wipe off the peroxide.

Before you begin, cover any surface with plastic that could be affected by the borax, like furniture, flooring, or carpeting.

Once a month wipe the area with straight distilled white vinegar to prevent the mold from returning. Vinegar stops mold from growing and the smell dissipates in a few hours.

Alternatively, you can mix 20 drops of grapefruit seed oil in 2 cups of water. Follow the directions above.

Moldy flooring is best treated by a professional.

The Least You Need to Know

- Invest in a CO detector for each level of your home, especially if you have woodburning stoves or fireplaces.

- Ventilation and plants help rid your home of air pollutants.

- Rather than use toxic air fresheners, try leaving cinnamon sticks or cloves in decorative dishes or use real flowers like lilies.

- It may take cleaning more often but the tidiness prevents allergies from worsening.

Chapter 17

Precision Speed Cleaning

In This Chapter

♦ Gather your tools

♦ Exercise reigns

♦ Time-tested tricks of the trade

♦ Divide and conquer

So you have better things to do than hang around the house with a rag in one hand and a spray bottle in the other? You want to zip through cleaning at neck breaking speed? Well, you don't need to throw your neck out of kilter just to speed clean the house. The tips in this chapter will get you whistling a happier tune.

I'm going to introduce you to a system I call Precision Cleaning. It encompasses all of my trade secrets to get you through these cleaning jobs—fast yet thoroughly. There is even a time table so you know how long it should take you to clean every piece of furniture and every item in your home.

Combine the time table with a bit of prep work, and you have a grasp on breakneck cleaning called Precision Cleaning.

Exercise and You

So you want the inside scoop to Precision Cleaning your home? Guess what? That trade secret is exercise. The better shape you are in, the more energy you have. The more energy you have, the faster you'll be zipping through all your daily routines. The health benefits you reap are immeasurable.

Mary's Handy Hints

Always check with your doctor if you have health issues. Pampering yourself with regular daily exercise is a whole body love hug. It's good for the heart and soul.

Work in a variety of exercise programs, aiming for 30–60 minutes every day. Alternate brisk walks with a variety of exercises like yoga, Pilates, and weight training to tone, condition, and exercise every muscle in your body.

Just how do you work in exercise when the kids have practice and you have club meetings? If necessary, get up 30 minutes earlier. Trust me, your energy level will be so much higher that you will never miss the 30 minutes of sleep. Admit it, the alarm goes off and you lay in bed for 30 minutes, right? We are all guilty—me too.

Here are a few ways to work in the exercise:

◆ Walk on your lunch hour.

◆ Call other parents to carpool the kids to practice.

◆ Use the warm-up time before your child's game to walk.

◆ Involve the entire family in an exercise program. Put up a basketball hoop, ride bikes, or join the community center.

Move It or Ditch It

Organizing. Ouch, even the most mature of us can throw a fit better than a two-year-old when it comes to being told to pick up our things.

A small cluttered home takes at least 90 minutes longer to clean than a well-organized home three times the size.

Try all you want, but without an organized home you aren't going anywhere except mud bogging with the monster trucks. Those trucks, like disorganization, usually end up spinning their wheels stuck in deep mucky muck.

Let's kick the clutter habit by running through some short and simple exercises. Organization is one of four building blocks to Precision Cleaning. The others are Prevention, Mary's Trade Secrets, and Knowing How to Clean the Right Way. Master these and you will be teaching the pros how to clean.

Organizational Keys

This section teaches you short basic steps to getting rid of most major clutter. Once the momentum starts to roll, you will adapt these techniques to declutter smaller areas, even drawers.

These are a few of the major clutter magnets in a home:

◆ Papers on the couch, magazines on the coffee table, and mail piled on the kitchen counter.

◆ Refrigerator full of month-old leftovers.

◆ Cabinets with out-of-date medicines or food.

◆ Clothing strung around the bedroom. Face it, you come home tired and hungry. The kids need attention, dinner waits, and hanging up clothes—well isn't that why they invented chairs?

Let's take a peek into a few quick preliminaries:

Prevention: Never leave a room empty-handed. Take something with you, put it away, toss it, or give it away.

Mary's trade secret: When you leave the bedroom, take the trash with you or a load of laundry down to wash. When you walk into the bedroom, grab a few pieces of clothing and hang them up.

Can't find closet space to hang clothes? Then spend an hour a week cleaning them. Some books recommend decluttering one room at a time. If I needed to declutter a home, it would lift my spirits to walk into any room and see progress. There is no right or wrong way to clear clutter—just the easy way. So go after clutter however it's fastest and easiest for you.

Shake it out: Don't shy away from change. Your home is cluttered because old habits continue to haunt you. Old habits caused the clutter, so toss them out with the old clothes and never look back.

Getting Started

First, make a date with yourself within the next day or two. Grab three boxes or large plastic bags. Box one are things to put away. Box two is the give away or garage sale box, and box three—yep—toss it.

Head from room to room and pick up one large pile from each room or the entire room, your choice. Immediately put away keepables, toss the trashables, and start a box for a garage sale or Goodwill. Make a date with yourself within the next three days to do it again. Keep your clutter dates and soon your home will look like the centerfold of *Home Beautiful*! Well, maybe not, but you will love the new roominess you have uncovered.

Tools of the Trade

When you need a job done, you gotta have tools. Here is a list of the tools to speed clean your way through all your chores:

◆ A big laundry basket to toss in anything that needs to be put away.

◆ A towel mop so you can dampen the towel and not have to carry around buckets of water or take time rinsing mops.

◆ A divided tote tray keeps your cleaning bottles and tools separated and easy to grab. Find them at hardware stores.

◆ A bottle of all-purpose cleaner.

◆ A bottle of glass cleaner.

◆ A lambswool duster.

◆ Rubber gloves to protect your hands.

- Baking soda.

- A dry sponge.

- A scraper.

- A stiff-bristled toothbrush.

- Add a lint roller if you have textured walls, popcorn ceilings, or wood beams. They remove cobwebs from rough surfaces.

The Basics

People today want fast. The fastest computers, instant dinners, problems resolved yesterday. Why should cleaning be any different? Cleaning so fast your vacuum cleaner smokes probably is not going to happen. With a few tricks, a smidge of practice, and conquering Precision Home Cleaning, you can cut most of the time spent cleaning by half if not more.

Clean like the pros: Professionals don't enter a home and heat up a cup of coffee, flip on the TV, or send an e-mail. When you clean, clean. Put everything else aside and stay focused. The answering machine can pick up phone messages—stay focused. Yes, I know with kids at home, this is not always possible. Engage your spouse to occupy the kids for a few hours if they are too young to help. If you are a single parent, plan to clean when the kids are out of the house. Better yet, put the kids to work.

Don't stop: You build speed as you clean. Every time you stop, it takes time to rebuild your momentum and costs you valuable time. Set your goal to clean the bathroom in 15 minutes and stay focused, and you will finish in that time.

New ways: Forget the old way of cleaning where you spray a small section of the surface, wipe it with one hand, and then pick up the bottle again to spray the next section. My Precision Method gets both hands in the act. Dampen two towels with your cleaner and then use the *Karate Kid* motions of "wax on wax off."

Your right hand moves counterclockwise and your left hand clockwise, so they overlap just enough to catch all the spots. Your surface will be cleared away before you start cleaning. Shortcuts to clearing surfaces are given as each room is covered.

Precision Home Cleaning is best achieved by cleaning your home in one day. If you find yourself doing a bit of cleaning each day, then do that one job completely. Dust the entire house or clean all the bathrooms. It takes time to pull out your cleaning equipment, so keep going until you finish.

Mary's Handy Hints

Each item in each room is timed. For instance, toilets take 45 seconds to clean. Use the charted time to tell you the areas where your time is lagging behind. Say, you are taking 90 seconds to clean a toilet but are cleaning sinks and showers faster. Your overall cleaning time is still on target. Study which areas are robbing your time and then reread that section to figure out how to speed up your time.

Divide and Conquer

Clean your home in sectors. Clean one sector and then move to the next. Adjust the following to the layout of your home.

Sector One: Bedrooms, bathrooms, and hallway area

Sector Two: Kitchen, eat-in section of the kitchen, den, and family room

Sector Three: Formal living room and dining room

Sector Four: Laundry room and remote rooms

Mary's Handy Hints

Add a 15- to 20-foot extension cord to your vacuum cleaner so you can reach all the rooms in one sector without taking time to move the cord from room to room.

Learning to do most anything usually means starting at the bottom and working your way to the top. I love breaking rules and this is one of them. You dust from the top down and start cleaning from the top floor of your home if you have more than one level. This keeps you from pulling dirt over freshly vacuumed floors.

On each floor begin with the rooms to the left, cleaning to the right. For one-story homes, begin with rooms on the far left and clean toward the center of the home, finishing with the rooms to the right. Carry a large garbage bag with you and empty the trash as you clean. A lot of clutter heads to the garbage with a trash bag in tow.

Are you with me so far? If not, e-mail me from my website and I'll answer your questions. Follow me through each sector.

Sector One: Bedrooms and Hallway

Start with the bedroom on the left of the hallway and work your way clockwise around the hallway. When I was professionally cleaning, this was the pattern I followed:

1. Clean the hall bathroom.

2. Clean the bathroom in the master bedroom.

3. Dust master bedroom.

4. Dust other bedrooms.

5. Dust hallway pictures and banister railing if there are steps.

6. Vacuum starting with the bedroom to the left and working around clockwise; then down the hallway and finally down the steps.

Why did I clean the bathrooms first rather than starting with the room on the left? Easy. I did them first because I was fresh and cleaned faster. Truthfully? I don't like cleaning bathrooms and did them first to get them out of the way.

Sector Two: Kitchen and Dinette Area, Den, and Family Room

Adjust these sectors for the layout of your home:

1. Dust the room at the back of this section, moving left to right if possible. If this sector includes a half bath, clean it as you dust the other rooms.

2. Dust hallway hangings.

3. Vacuum beginning from left to right, finishing by backing down a corridor or the hallway.

4. Clean the kitchen table and any wall hangings in the kitchen area.

Clean the kitchen as described in Chapter 6.

Sector Three: Formal Living and Dining Room, Office, or Den

1. Dust the room to the left, moving across the foyer if there is one.

2. Finish dusting any other room.

3. Clean any bathroom in this sector.

4. Vacuum each room and the entryway.

5. Damp-mop the entryway.

Sector Four: Laundry Room and Remote Rooms

This sector can vary so widely I can never give all the examples possible. Your washer and dryer might be out in the garage. Or you might have a sun room or a craft room. If those rooms are close to Sector Three, you might want to clean them with Sector Three.

Clean this sector following the same pattern in Sector Two.

Time It

The night before cleaning, move objects on tables or desks to the far right or place them on a nearby sofa or chair.

On cleaning day as you clear breakfast dishes, place any placemats, napkin holders, and so forth on the seats of the dining room chairs. Each member of the family should be responsible for moving their own placemat, even the kids.

Precision dusting: Grab a cotton tube sock (an older but "holy" one is just fine as long as it is clean and doesn't smell like your son's sneakers). Place this sock on your dominant hand that will move objects. Spray it down with your furniture cleaner.

The other hand works with a diaper cloth or a 100 percent cotton soft cloth like a white T-shirt. Spray it as well with the furniture cleaner and conditioner.

Dusting is one amazing way to work in a good aerobic workout while cleaning, so let's get funky with dusting. Both hands are used, which increases blood circulation. Remember wipe on wipe off. Use it for dusting as well.

Chairs: Squat behind the chair and dust down each leg and the rungs with the corresponding hand—one on each side of the chair. Then come up the sides of the back and across the back and the front, still using both hands. It takes a little bit of practice. You will soon master it. Time? 10 seconds.

End tables: Bring your socked hand down the base of the lamp and then pick it up as your other hand dusts underneath the lamp. Continue lifting objects with the socked hand and dusting with the baby diaper cloth. Use both hands to dust down the legs. Time? 15 seconds.

Coffee tables: Use the same method used for dusting end tables. Start at the left side of the coffee table again with your right hand working counterclockwise and your left hand clockwise. Squat down as far as necessary and go. Time? 10 seconds.

Dining room table: Work the same way as a coffee table. Spray the table first if any food is stuck on the table. Time? One minute 30 seconds.

Dressers and chest of drawers: Keep as few objects on your dresser as possible. Larger objects such as jewelry cases are easy to move and dust; it's the small stuff that counts—time wise, that is. Dust the top starting at the left and working your way over mirrors using the double-handed method. When you finish the top, dust the lower-right side, work your way across the front, and finish with the left side. Time? 2 minutes.

Remember to spray a lint-free towel with a bit of window cleaner and tuck it into your back pocket. Grab the cloth with your socked hand, clean the mirror, and keep going.

General Dusting Patterns

No matter what room you are cleaning, the flow is from top to bottom, left to right. Begin at the left of the room. Dust any wall hangings first and then any table, chair, or other piece of furniture immediately beneath it. By dusting the higher areas first, any dust that might float down doesn't dirty up the surface you just cleaned.

Move furniture away from the wall as you dust. It saves 10 minutes per room moving furniture when you start to vacuum.

General Vacuuming Patterns

Start vacuuming the first room you dusted in each sector. You moved the furniture out as you dusted. Right? If not, pull the furniture out from the walls two widths of your vacuum cleaner. You will make two swipes at the carpet behind the furniture.

Begin at the left and vacuum behind the furniture following close to the baseboard. Return the furniture. Vacuum the middle of the room and then behind the furniture on the right side. Replace the furniture and vacuum your way out the door.

Precision Clean Your Bathroom

Me? Enjoy cleaning bathrooms? Right and one-legged ducks don't swim in circles. Soap scum builds in the shower and rings in the toilet run rampart because it's so easy to find other things to do than clean the bathroom. With a few new ideas and fresh approaches, you will be in and out of there in 12–15 minutes for an average-size bathroom. Reread Chapter 7 for important preventive tips.

Prepare for Battle

We grew up learning to prepare for everything we did. We practiced the piano and studied for exams and took driver's education. Well, cleaning is no exception. Do a bit of prep work to save hours of cleaning time:

- On the morning you are going to clean the bathroom, put every-thing on top of the counter away in a drawer or cabinet as you brush your teeth. Time? 0 seconds.

- When you finish brushing your teeth, fill the sink with hot water. Place your soap dishes in the sink to soak. The hot water soaks the soap residue off the soap dishes. The soap residue in turn cleans the sink. Time? 30 seconds.

- Gather your cleaning gear and pull out your color-coded terry towels for the bathroom, which are blue in the Precision Cleaning Kit.

Ready, Set, Go

The bathroom is the one area you might not clean left to right because of the layout of the room. First, clean the sink area; then the toilet, shower, or tub; finishing with the floor.

Start by sprinkling a small bit of baking soda inside the toilet. Pick up your diluted bottle of Red Juice by The Clean Team, CleanEz, or organic cleaner and pour some onto both of the towels. Do spray the toilet inside and outside rather than wiping it.

Next, wipe down the counter and faucet and pour more cleaner on your towels. Wipe down the shower starting at the bottom of the left side of the shower door if there is one and working your way to the top by moving clockwise around the shower. Time? 4 minutes.

Finally, grab your window cleaner and spray some into a lint-free towel like an old cotton T-shirt. Wipe the mirror. Time? 15 seconds.

NOTE: If you soaked your soap dishes in the sink when you finished brushing your teeth, you will use the water and soap already in the sink to clean it rather than spraying the sink.

Scrub your toilet with your scrub brush and rinse it by scrubbing the sink—remember that the sink is full of soapy water. Let the water out of the sink. Time? 45 seconds.

Now we go ambidextrous and use both hands to clean. Use a lint-free towel in both hands to clean the mirror. If you don't remember the hand motions, reread the section "The Basics" to learn how to work your hands. Time? 10 seconds.

Next, grab the two color-coded bathroom towels, one in each hand. Use the dry sides of the towels. The left hand wipes the left side of the counter and left part of the sink, while the right hand does the right side. It may take a time or two to get used to using both hands. Once you get the hang of this, though, you'll never clean any other way. And it's a good workout as well! Time? 1 minute and 15 seconds.

Next up is the toilet. Again, use both hands to clean their respective sides. Wipe the toilet tank, cover, seats, down the outside, and around the back. Time? 30 seconds.

The showers are next. Continue with both hands and start with the sliding glass door if you have one, working from left to right, top to bottom. Continue around the shower or tub, moving to the right and cleaning top to bottom. Time? 3 minutes and 30 seconds.

Spray the bottom of the shower and then dampen the green floor towel to clean the floor. Scrub the bottom of the tub or shower and mop your way out of the bathroom. Time? 2 minutes.

Total Time? 12–15 minutes for an average-size bathroom.

Sleeping Quarters

You have the basics of dusting mastered by now, right? If not? Well ... I don't make house calls, so reread this chapter.

If you are cleaning the master bedroom or another bedroom with an attached bathroom, clean the bathroom first and then dust, finishing with the vacuuming.

 Dirty Words

Prevent your wood furniture from drying and cracking by applying a wood conditioner at least once a year.

Remember: Dust high areas first, which includes the ceiling. Use your lambswool duster or towel over your towel mop to snatch those cobwebs.

Now you are ready to start Precision Cleaning bedrooms. Start at the left side of the room, dusting wall hangings followed by any furniture below them continuing clockwise around the room. See the individual pieces in the previous sections for Precise Cleaning methods.

Dust window sills as you come to those and mini blinds when they come up on the schedule.

To vacuum, start at the back left side of the bedroom and work your way around beds, dressers, and sleeping dogs. Vacuum the closet as you come to that point, working your way out the door.

K. P. Duty

If cleaning the bathroom brought on the blues, then K. P. duty will not get you singing happy tunes either. It does help to turn on some upbeat music such as calypso or whatever keeps your mind off cleaning and your body moving quickly. This is not the time to play soft, gently swaying music. Save that for a cup of tea and a well-deserved rest when you finish.

Grab your color-coded kitchen towels. Precision Cleaning Kit towels are white if you want to follow the pattern.

Prep Work

As you are cleaning up the dishes the night before cleaning the kitchen, tuck "things" away in a cabinet. Time? 2 minutes and 30 seconds.

Ready, Set, Go

Begin by placing a microwaveable cup half filled with water into the microwave and heating it for 3 minutes. Pour a bit of the boiling water from the coffee cup onto any stuck-on food spots on top of the stove. Add a drop of liquid dish soap. Time? 45 seconds.

Spray the entire top of your stove with your cleaner to give the tough stuff ample time to soften. Time? 5 seconds.

Start at the left side and move all objects on the counter to the right as far as possible. Open areas encourage cleaning because you can clean them quickly. Time? 1 minute and 30 seconds.

Pour your organic cleaner on one end of both kitchen cleaning towels. Guess what? This is where we get funky with both hands again. Place one towel in each hand. Using the same "wax on wax off" motion by starting at the left and working to the right. Wipe down the dishwasher as you come to it, using both hands.

Dirty Words _____

Never use regular cleaners on tile, marble, granite, or other stone surfaces. They will damage the surface. Use hot water only and Nature's Miracle to disinfect them.

You can use only one hand to clean the microwave, but it goes quickly because you have the surface pre-treated. Time? 5 minutes.

Clean those cabinets: Pour a bit of vinegar and water onto a cloth to wipe down the door knobs of the cabinets. Clean one section of the cabinets each week to keep ahead of the grime. Pay special attention to door knobs. Time? 5 minutes.

Refrigerator: Next, tackle the refrigerator. Dampen your cloths again. Grab a chair to reach the top. Clean the top and start wiping down the front using both hands, always starting at the top. Finish by cleaning the inside gaskets and exposed areas that need attention. Time? 3 minutes and 15 seconds.

Stove: Remove the burners and drip pans. Wipe the front of the stove using both hands. Time? 4 minutes.

You presprayed the top of the stove, so wipe it down next. An SOS pad still seems to be the best way to clean drip pans. Use a rubber mat in your sink to prevent scratching. Dampen the drip pans with hot water and soak the SOS pad just a bit. Add the needed elbow grease and then rinse. Time? 5–6 minutes.

Congratulations! The kitchen sparkles. But don't pick up that cup of tea yet. You still must do the floor and sink. Clean the floor first, following the directions in Chapter 10. Then do the sink, following directions in Chapter 6. Time? Varies.

Living Room, Family Room, Dining Room, et al.

Reread the general dusting guidelines at the beginning of this chapter to review step-by-step how to dust. Follow the same left-to-right dusting discussed in the section "Sleeping Quarters." Remember to spray down your lint-free towel with glass cleaner (tuck it into your back pocket) to clean any glass.

After you have dusted the room, vacuum as discussed in the section "General Vacuuming Patterns."

For hard floor surfaces, vacuum, dust, and mop using the same pattern outlined previously. By now, you have gained enough information to adapt the general cleaning technique to any room in your home if it is not specifically covered.

The Least You Need to Know

- If you look at housework as being drudgery; it will be just that.
- Keep your bottles filled and all supplies in one place.
- Using both hands to clean may require some adjustments but once you do adjust to this new method there is no going back to old ways.
- Always engage family members when it comes to doing chores but remember to have fun.

A

Your Complete Stain-Removal Guide

So you spilled something on something else. No worries! This appendix tells you how to get just about any substance off of just about any surface with Earth- and human-friendly methods.

General Guidelines

Let's set a few guidelines before you start blotting and wiping:

◆ Always test an inconspicuous spot for color fastness before you go all out on the stain.

◆ Give your product time to work. Apply the cleaner and allow it to set undisturbed for 15 minutes.

◆ Bi-O-Kleen and CleanEz both remove most stains. Never use petroleum distillates, which may be listed as mineral spirits, aliphatic hydrocarbon, hydrocarbon, or other known harsh chemicals listed in The Hit List.

◆ Clean a spill immediately. The longer it sets, the harder it is to remove the stain.

◆ Use a clean white rag to remove stains. The color from a rag can transfer onto the surface you're cleaning.

- Frequently move the cloth so that a clean surface is showing to keep the stain from spreading.

- On fabrics, begin spraying the cleaner from the outer edges of the stain and work your way toward the center of the stain. This keeps the stain from spreading.

- Keep a bottle of enzyme cleaner such as Nature's Miracle on hand for cleaning urine, vomit, and all organic stains. By the time you run out to the store to buy a bottle, the stain can set!

These tips can save you a lot of work, giving you more time to sip lemonade and relax on your porch swing.

Carpet Stain-Removal Guidelines

Follow these guidelines when removing carpet stains:

- Always blot; never rub. Rubbing breaks down the fibers and weakens the material.

- Blot by punching your index knuckle into a rag dampened with $\frac{1}{4}$ cup white vinegar per quart of water. Start with your wrist facing to the right, twisting clockwise. Carpet fibers are twisted clockwise. This motion prevents fuzzy spots.

- When liquid spills into carpet, it hits the padding and spreads. You must clean an area of carpet twice as large as the surface stain when more than 2 ounces of liquid has spilled.

- For larger spills, use a wet or dry vacuum or Bissell type vacuum if available to suck up as much liquid as possible. Otherwise place two to three terry towels on top of the stain then walk on the stain, wearing shoes of course, to absorb the liquid. Replace the towels as they become saturated.

- Work carefully with peroxide. Let it set 15 minutes and rinse with $\frac{1}{4}$ cup vinegar per quart of water. Many carpets are made from Olefin. Peroxide can remove the dye in these carpets.

- Rinse any cleaner with $\frac{1}{4}$ cup white vinegar per quart of water taking care not to oversaturate the carpet.

Now, on to the good stuff!

Stain-Removal Secrets

Beer on the upholstery? Soot on the walls? Mascara on the carpet? (Hey, it happens.) Here's the lowdown on the stains.

Ballpoint Ink

Carpet: Apply rubbing alcohol with a cotton swab to prevent the stain from spreading. Wait 15 minutes, blot, and repeat if necessary. Rinse.

Fabric furniture and mattresses: Try a squirt of white foaming shaving cream. Spray on enough to cover the spot and wait 30 minutes. Wipe off the excess and rinse.

Laminated/wood floor and wood furniture: Apply a dab of rubbing alcohol, wait five minutes, then wipe. Repeat if needed. If this does not work, try white (not gel) foaming shaving cream.

Leather/vinyl: Use only products made specifically for leather, like Leather Care or a beeswax-based cleaner. Anything else can dry and crack the leather.

 Dirty Words

You may read recommendations to use hairspray for ink removal. Hairspray contains alcohol, which removes the ink. The other chemicals in hairspray could damage a fabric, though. Use caution with hairspray.

Linoleum floors: Rub with a bit of toothpaste.

Walls: Rub with a bit of toothpaste or seal and paint the spot.

Beer and Alcohol

Carpet: Blot the stain. Apply Nature's Miracle, an enzyme cleaner; wait an hour or more; and rinse with plain water.

Fabric furniture: Follow the manufacturer's guidelines. Remove the cushion and rinse in 1 gallon of cool water plus $1/2$ cup of white vinegar. Soak the foam in the tub, using the previously mentioned formula. Air dry it, keeping the cushion stretched to prevent shrinking. Or wash the entire cushion in the tub if it is washable.

Laminated/wood floor: Wipe with $1/4$ cup of white vinegar per quart of water. Dry and run a fan to finish drying the floor. Contact the manufacturer for the proper method to restore the wood should it discolor. If the wood warps, sand and refinish the floor. You cannot sand and refinish laminated floors, though.

Leather/vinyl: Wipe with an enzyme cleaner like Nature's Miracle. Wait 24 hours and repeat if needed. Apply a high-quality leather and vinyl conditioner to prevent drying.

Linoleum: Remove excess moisture. Clean the floor with Nature's Miracle and rinse with plain water. Dry immediately.

Mattresses: Professionally clean to remove the odor and stain.

Tile, marble, granite floors: See linoleum.

Walls: Clean with Bi-O-Kleen or Seventh Generation liquid dish soap using minimal water. Rinse with straight vinegar.

Wood furniture: Liquid spills darken and possibly warp the wood. Clean with $1/4$ cup white vinegar per quart of water. Dry. If the wood has darkened, sand and refinish the furniture. If the wood has not darkened, apply a high-quality wood conditioner.

Berry Stains

Carpet, upholstery, and mattresses: Use straight 3 percent hydrogen peroxide; wait 20 minutes. Rinse. Repeat if needed after 24 hours. Or use 1 teaspoon borax per quart of water.

Laminated/wood floor: Sand and refinish wood floors because the stain will not come out. Use peroxide on laminated floors.

Leather/vinyl: This stain may not come out. Try blotting with hydrogen peroxide, letting it soak an hour keeping the towel damp. Hold the towel in place with a bowl. Rinse with plain water and dry. Follow with a leather/vinyl conditioner.

Tile, marble, granite floors: The StainEraser is the only item that will remove berry stains from grout.

Walls: Mix a paste of peroxide and baking soda. Dab on and wait 30 minutes. Blot to remove. Seal and paint if needed.

Wood furniture: Use 3 percent peroxide with caution because it can bleach the wood. Apply, wait 5 minutes, and blot with ¼ cup white vinegar per quart of water. Use the meat of a walnut or pecan to restore the color if needed. Treat with wood conditioner.

Blood

Carpet and upholstery: Blot with Nature's Miracle or a 50/50 solution cool water and 3 percent peroxide. Rinse.

Wood/laminated floors and wood furniture: Blood is difficult to remove because it darkens wood. Lighten the stain with peroxide using caution. Blot with ¼ cup vinegar to 1 quart cool water.

Leather/vinyl: Clean with cold water or 3 percent peroxide.

Mattresses: Blot with an enzyme cleaner or 3 percent peroxide.

Tile, marble, granite floors: For white grout, spray with 3 percent peroxide. For colored grout, rinse with cold water, dry, and then use The StainEraser to remove the rest.

Walls: Blot with 3 percent peroxide.

Dirty Words

Wear rubber gloves when cleaning another person's blood, even if it's a close friend or family member. Hepatitis C and other diseases are spread by blood contact; the person might not know he is a carrier because some diseases can take years to discover.

Chocolate

Carpet: Dab with a bit of nonalkali organic liquid dish soap, and wait 30 minutes. Rinse and repeat if needed. Use a 50/50 solution of hydrogen peroxide to water if any stain remains.

Fabric furniture: Use white foaming shaving cream. Rinse.

Grout in stone flooring: Use white foaming shaving cream. Spray on, wait at least 15 minutes, and wipe up.

Walls: Dab on a nonalkali liquid dishwashing detergent. Rinse using as little moisture as possible.

Wood furniture: See the section "Grease (Auto) and Motor Oil."

Coffee or Cola

Carpet: For large spills, follow the advice in the "Carpet Stain-Removal Guidelines." Otherwise, blot with a 50/50 solution of peroxide to water. Rinse. Or dilute 1 tablespoon borax per quart of water, blot, and rinse.

Fabric furniture and mattresses: Spray on white foaming shaving cream, wait 15–20 minutes, and rinse.

Laminated/wood floor and wood furniture: Wipe immediately. If water spots remain, rub in a bit of real mayonnaise.

Tile, marble, granite floors: Use The StainEraser.

Walls: Blot on 3 percent hydrogen peroxide. Repeat every 30 minutes until the stain is gone.

Cooking Oil (Including Bacon, Butter, and Lard)

See the section "Grease (Auto) and Motor Oil."

Crayon

Carpet and upholstery: Freeze the crayon with an ice cube tucked into a Ziploc bag. Scrape off what you can with a blunt knife. Use a concentrated organic cleaner like CleanEz or Bi-O-Kleen to remove the rest. Rub a bit into the carpet, twisting clockwise with your index finger and thumb. Wait 30 minutes and rinse with vinegar and water.

Be careful not to work the cleaner down to the backing. Degreasing cleaners like CleanEz or Bi-O-Kleen can dissolve the adhesive holding the fibers to the pad.

Mattresses: Use undiluted concentrated organic cleaner to remove anything that remains after freezing. Apply with a cotton swab, wait 15–30 minutes, and gently blot. You may need to rinse several times.

Laminated/wood floor: Freeze the crayon with an ice cube tucked into a Ziploc bag. Carefully scrape off what you can with a plastic scraper. Use a hair dryer to heat the crayon, dabbing with a cloth as it melts. Do NOT overheat the flooring or push the crayon into the seams. Never use an iron on any surface.

Leather/vinyl: Use a mild solvent such as DeSolvIt. Wipe on, wait 10 minutes, and blot. Rinse with organic dish soap and then with plain water. Apply a conditioner such as Leather Care.

Linoleum: Freeze with ice and chip off what you can with a blunt knife. Finish with DeSolvIt or a concentrated organic cleaner.

Tile, marble, granite: See laminated floors. Do not use a solvent.

Walls: Do not use a solvent because it will stain and prevent paint from sticking to the wall. Dip a cloth in boiling hot water with a bit of liquid dish soap. Blot only. Apply a primer and paint over it if necessary.

Wood furniture: For hard, slick finishes, blot with a clean cloth and heat with a hair dryer, wiping with a cloth. Call a refinisher for antique furniture. For tung oil finishes, freeze with ice and scrape off what you can. Use a hair dryer and clean cloth to remove the rest.

Dirt

Carpet, mattresses, and upholstery: Blot with an organic all-purpose cleaner and rinse with vinegar and water.

Laminated/wood floor and wood furniture: Clean with $\frac{1}{4}$ cup white vinegar to 1 quart of water.

Mary's Handy Hints

If your dirt begins as mud, allow it to dry and then brush or vacuum away what you can before using a cleaner.

Walls: Wipe the dirt off with an organic cleaner.

Dye

Dye will not come out of leather, vinyl, hard floor surfaces, mattresses, walls, wood, or clothing.

Carpet and upholstery: *Red dye 40 (found in dog and cat food, popsicles, Kool-Aid, and punch):* Blot with 3 percent peroxide. Wait 15 minutes; rinse. *Hair dye:* Call a carpet-cleaning company because anything you do will only spread the stain.

Grout: If The StainEraser doesn't take it out, nothing will.

Feces

Carpet and upholstery: Remove with an enzyme product like Nature's Miracle. Follow the bottle's directions.

Laminated/wood floor: Use minimal amounts of enzyme cleaner. Wipe on, wait 5 minutes, and rinse with $\frac{1}{4}$ cup white vinegar per quart of water. Dry immediately.

Leather/vinyl: Use an enzyme product. Follow the bottle's directions.

Linoleum: Use an enzyme product, following the bottle's directions.

Mattresses: Professionally clean it.

Tile, marble, granite floors: Use an enzyme product, following the instructions on the label.

Food

Refer to the specific stain.

Glue and Adhesives

Carpet and mattresses: See the section "Crayon."

Laminated/wood floor, wood furniture, tile, marble, granite: Freeze and treat as for crayon in carpet. Dab on a bit of smooth peanut butter, wait 5 minutes, and blot. Sometimes peanut butter oil dissolves the glue. Or call a flooring specialist.

Leather/vinyl: Good luck. This one is rough because the glue works down into these fabrics and is quite tough to remove. Treat as you would for crayon.

Linoleum and walls: See the section "Crayon."

Grease (Auto) and Motor Oil

Carpet: Dab on rubbing alcohol with a cotton swab. Wait 15–20 minutes and blot. If this does not work, use an undiluted organic cleaner working it into the fibers by twisting the fibers clockwise between your finger and thumb. Use caution not to work the orange cleaner near the base of the carpet because it will dissolve the adhesive that holds the fibers to the padding. Wait 30 minutes and blot. Rinse with $\frac{1}{4}$ cup vinegar per quart of water.

Fabric furniture: White foaming shaving cream works best. Spray on, wait 5–10 minutes, and rinse with vinegar and water.

Laminated/wood floor and wood furniture: Blot with a soft cloth like an old clean cotton T-shirt. Apply a dab of rubbing alcohol. Wait no longer than 5 minutes, rinsing with ¼ cup white vinegar per quart of water.

Leather/vinyl: Spray on white foaming shaving cream, wait 15–20 minutes, gently rub with a soft cloth, and rinse with plain water. Always follow with a good-quality leather cleaner and conditioner, such as Leather Care.

Linoleum: Spray on rubbing alcohol or white foaming shaving cream; let it set 10–15 minutes. Rinse with water.

Mattresses: Use white foaming shaving cream; apply, let it set for 15 minutes, and blot.

Tile, marble, granite floors: Wipe with a clean, soft cloth. Try white foaming shaving cream first, letting it set 10 minutes. Blot and rinse. Or mix a paste of rubbing alcohol and baking soda. Apply, wait 10 minutes, and rinse. (Do not use on granite or marble.)

Walls: Mix a paste of rubbing alcohol and cornstarch. Plaster on the spot. Let it set 45 minutes and dry. Apply a paint primer, and then touch up the spot with leftover paint.

Wood furniture: Rubbing alcohol will remove grease and oil from sealed furniture. Apply, wait no longer than 5 minutes, and dry with a soft cloth. For tung oil finishes, press cornstarch into the wood. Wait 30–60 minutes and vacuum off the cornstarch. Keep applying until no more oil is absorbed. Then dab on a bit of rubbing alcohol, following the previously mentioned directions. Apply furniture wax to the entire surface to restore the luster.

Gum

Here's the general rule for removing gum from any surface: freeze the gum with a cube of ice in a zippered plastic bag. Use a plastic scraper to chip away all you can. Repeat until most of the gum has been removed, and then follow the directions for your surface.

Follow the directions for crayon to remove the rest.

Hair Dye

See the section "Dye."

Hand Lotion

Carpet and upholstery: Dab with organic dish soap and rinse.

Laminated/wood floor and wood furniture: Work cornstarch into the wood; then wait 30 minutes. Vacuum the cornstarch and repeat until the oil is absorbed. Remove the rest with rubbing alcohol. Let it set no longer than 5 minutes, rinse, and dry. Beeswax restores the luster in wood furniture.

Leather/vinyl: Absorb what you can with cornstarch. If any lotion remains, blot on white foaming shaving cream. Wait 5 minutes, and rinse with ¼ cup white vinegar per quart of water.

Linoleum: Clean with an organic all-purpose cleaner.

Mattresses: Use an organic all-purpose cleaner.

Tile, marble, granite floors: Wipe with a clean cloth and hot water.

Walls: Mix a paste of cornstarch and water and plaster the spot. Wait 30 minutes and wipe off. Lotion leaves a stain, so use a primer and then paint.

Iodine and Metholide

Carpet, upholstery, and mattresses: Rinse with cool water, working from the outer area toward the center. Blot, turning the towel often. Remove the rest with hydrogen peroxide; then rinse.

Laminated/wood floor and wood furniture: Use cool water only. Sand and refinish if the stain remains—and it probably will.

Leather/vinyl: White foaming shaving cream might work. Dab on, wait 15 minutes, and rinse with cool water.

Linoleum: Use cool water. If the iodine or metholide seeps into the sublayers, the stain will be permanently set.

Tile, marble, granite floors: Blot with cool water.

Walls: Blot with cool water. Prime and repaint if needed.

Juice

See the next section, "Kool-Aid, Popsicles, Punch, and Grape Juice."

Kool-Aid, Popsicles, Punch, and Grape Juice

These stains are all caused by red dye 40, except for grape juice, but they're treated the same way. Immediately sponge 3 percent peroxide onto the spot and let it set for 15–20 minutes. Rinse. This treatment may also work for wood, but it can take the color out. If this happens, rub it with the meat of a walnut or pecan or use a stain.

Lipstick

Treat as you would for grease and motor oil.

Magic Marker

When the label reads *permanent*, that means *permanent*. Repeated cleaning sometimes removes the stain—maybe.

Carpet, fabric furniture, and mattresses: Mix 1 teaspoon of borax and a drop of organic dish soap with 1 cup of lukewarm water. Blot, wait 10 minutes, and rinse.

Laminated/wood floor and wood furniture: Sand the wood with very fine sandpaper. Then use a wood conditioner to restore the wood.

Tile: Spray with Motsenbocker's Lift Off #3. Spray, wait 1 minute, and then wipe with a clean towel. Repeat if necessary.

Leather/vinyl: Good luck! Try foaming shaving cream.

Walls: Sorry! Apply a primer and repaint the spot.

Mascara and Makeup

Carpet and fabric furniture: Pour a dab of organic dish soap onto a damp clean cloth. Blot on, wait 10 minutes, and rinse with vinegar and water.

Corian or marble bathroom counters: Clean with hot water or a bit of white foaming shaving cream.

Merthiolate

See the section "Iodine and Metholide."

Milk

Carpet, fabric furniture, and mattresses: Mix one part white vinegar to four parts water, or use Nature's Miracle. Saturate the carpet, wait 30 minutes, and rinse.

Laminated floors: Use ¼ cup white vinegar per quart of water.

Wood floors: Wipe it; then walk on a terry towel to pull the moisture into the towel. Clean the floor with Nature's Miracle, rinse, and dry. Set a fan on the floor to dry the boards.

Wood furniture: Follow the steps for a wood floor, but eliminate the fan. Dry thoroughly. Apply a good wood cleaner and conditioner.

Leather/vinyl: Wipe with a 50/50 solution of white vinegar to warm water; then finish with a leather/vinyl conditioner.

Linoleum: Use ¼ cup white vinegar per quart of water.

Marble, tile, and granite: Use hot water only or Nature's Miracle.

Walls: Clean with an organic all-purpose cleaner.

Mold/Mildew

Bathroom ceilings, tile, and grout: Mix a solution of 50/50 white vinegar to water. Clean the mold and allow it to dry. Then clean with 25 percent food-grade hydrogen peroxide (found at health food stores). Borax also works but not as effectively. Mix ¼ cup per quart of warm water. Wait 24 hours and repeat if necessary.

Wood furniture: Sanding and refinishing the wood is the best treatment for moldy wood.

Decks, siding, and roofs: Rent a power washer and clean the deck. Allow it to dry and clean with a 50/50 solution of vinegar to water to kill the mold. Stain and seal the deck to prevent mold.

Carpet: Always be cautious of mold in carpet and walls. It could be a toxic mold. Hire a carpet company specializing in remediation to clean moldy carpet. Call a local janitorial supply store for recommendations.

For small spots, clean with 50/50 solution vinegar to water. Keep a fan on the spot to dry the carpet. Pull the carpet back and treat and seal the floor. It might be wise to replace the carpet. Use a dehumidifier to eliminate further mold.

Fabric furniture: Take the furniture outdoors (to prevent the mold from spreading in the home), and brush off any visible mold. Wash the broom with straight vinegar before reusing.

Then clean with a vacuum cleaner and attachment brush again, cleaning the brush with vinegar. Dispose of the bag or empty the bag outdoors; then clean it with vinegar to prevent scattering the mold indoors.

Mattresses: Spray the mattress first with 50/50 solution vinegar to water and then with 25 percent food-grade peroxide (found in health food stores). Then let the mattress set in the sun all day, turning it once to expose both sides to the sunlight.

Laminated/wood floor: *For waxed finish:* The mold can usually be removed with a wood floor cleaning liquid and No. 1 steel wool.

For surface finishes: If mold is on the surface, wipe up with 50/50 vinegar to water. You may need to refinish the floor.

Linoleum: Gray splotchy areas indicate mold growing from the floor-boards. Find the source of the moisture and treat it immediately. Nothing kills this mold. Unfortunately, the floor must be replaced.

Leather/vinyl: Wipe with a cloth moistened with 50/50 vinegar to water, turning on a fan to dry it. Then clean with 3 percent peroxide, dry, and treat with a conditioner.

Mustard

See the section "Coffee or Cola."

Nail Polish

As green as I try to be, some stains simply require the use of a toxic cleaner. Nail polish is one of them.

Carpet, fabric furniture, and mattresses: Apply nonacetone nail polish remover and blot. Mix 1 teaspoon of an organic cleaner—no bleaches—with a cup of lukewarm water and blot. Rinse.

Laminated/wood floor: Rub gently with steel wool. Rinse, dry completely, and recoat with appropriate finish or wax if needed.

Leather/vinyl: There are now so many new varieties of vinyl and leather finishes that it is best to call the manufacturer for removal instructions. What might work for one type of vinyl or leather might damage another.

Linoleum: Follow the bottle's directions using a clean white cloth and fingernail polish remover containing acetone. Finish by rinsing with sudsy water. The stain is permanent and won't come out. You might need to wax the floor if the acetone removes the wax.

Tile, marble, and granite floors: Spray with Motsenbocker's Lift Off #3. Spray the stain thoroughly, wait at least 60 seconds, and then wipe with a clean towel. Repeat if necessary.

Walls: Spray with Motsenbocker's Lift Off #3 (found at Home Depot and True Value hardware stores). Saturate the stain, wait 1 minute, and wipe with a clean towel. Repeat if necessary.

Wood furniture: Avoid nail polish remover because the solvents will ruin wood finishes. Remove wet nail polish with mineral spirits. If dry, soak the stain for 2–3 minutes with boiled linseed oil; then scrape off the residue with a nonstick spatula. Allow it to dry and treat with a wood conditioner to prevent drying.

Ointments

See the section "Grease (Auto) and Motor Oil."

Paste Wax

Use your concentrated organic cleaner to dissolve the residue. If that does not work, hardware stores carry a product called DeSolvIt that works well on most surfaces.

Blot on the cleaner, wait 1 hour, and blot. Rinse with liquid dish soap and then with vinegar and water.

For wood furniture and wood flooring, contact a professional.

Paint: Latex, Water-Based Paints, and Art Paint

Carpet: Moisten with hot water. Spray on white foaming shaving cream and let it set several hours. Blot and then rinse. When the paint is softening, blot and reapply if needed. Rinse.

Fabric furniture and mattresses: Mix 1 teaspoon of a mild detergent containing no alkalis or bleaches with a cup of lukewarm water and blot it on the stain. Rinse. White foaming shaving cream will also work.

Laminated/wood floor: Scrub with a concentrated solution of detergent and water.

Leather/vinyl: Use denatured alcohol or white foaming shaving cream, following the instructions for carpet.

Linoleum: Rub with a cloth or plastic mesh pad dipped in warm water and detergent.

Tile, marble, and granite floors: Scrape off what you can with a plastic scraper, and then apply very hot water with a cloth, adding elbow grease. The StainEraser will remove paint from grout.

Pencil

Carpet, fabric furniture, and mattresses: First use a piece of boxing tape—not duct tape—doubled over to lift off as much of the pencil as possible. Then use a soft art eraser (the kind that can be molded, not a gum eraser). Rub it over the stain very gently; it should lift the pencil mark out. If any remains, clean with liquid dishwashing soap, blot, and rinse.

Tile, marble, and granite floors: Rub gently with an art gum eraser.

Laminated/wood floor: Rub gently with an art gum eraser.

Leather/vinyl: Rub gently with an art gum eraser.

Linoleum: Rub gently with an art gum eraser.

Walls: Rub gently with an art gum eraser.

Wood furniture: Rub gently with an art gum eraser.

Wallpaper: Rub gently with an art gum eraser or commercial wallpaper cleaner. On washable paper, wipe with damp sponge or sudsy sponge and then damp sponge if needed to remove the mark.

Petroleum Jelly

See the section "Grease (Auto) and Motor Oil."

Popsicles and Punch

See the section "Kool-Aid, Popsicles, Punch, and Grape Juice."

Rubber-Backed Throw Rugs

Unfortunately, the yellow stains left by these rugs on any floor surface are permanent. We recommend using only light-colored 100 percent cotton throw rugs with nonslip padding underneath them. If you do use these carpets, pick them up whenever any moisture lands on the carpet. Always pick them up after you shower and at night if they are in the kitchen. Watch closely for early signs of yellowing.

Rust

Carpet, fabric furniture, and mattresses: Squeeze enough juice from a fresh lemon to thoroughly saturate the spot. Generously sprinkle on some salt and let that set 24 hours, refreshing the lemon juice once or twice during that time. Rinse with cool water and repeat if needed.

Metal surfaces: Treat metal immediately. It's easier to treat a small spot than to sand and repaint. Naval jelly dissolves small rust spots. Naval jelly contains phosphoric acid, which is toxic. It might be necessary to use navel jelly to properly prepare a metal surface for paint. Another product called Rusterizer claims to be organic and an effective rust remover. After the rust has been removed, rinse with sudsy water, dry thoroughly, and paint with a rust preventive paint.

Porcelain and fiberglass: Rub the stain with a cut lemon, or apply lemon juice. Alternatively, boil distilled white vinegar then soak a heavy duty paper towel in the vinegar. First, sponge the vinegar on the rust then place the towel on top of the stain. Keep the towel wet with hot vinegar for several hours. Scrub with a salt and vinegar paste. Rinse thoroughly with hot water and paint to prevent the rust from returning.

Laminated/wood floor and linoleum: First try lemon juice leaving it on the spot for only a few minutes. Preferably call the floor manufacturer for recommendations. If steel wool is suggested, use 000 grade.

Leather/vinyl: Treat as you would for carpet. Rinse thoroughly and finish with a leather/vinyl conditioner.

Tile, marble, and granite floors: Squeeze lemon juice on the spot for a few minutes. Rub gently with salt and lemon juice paste. Rinse immediately. Do not leave the lemon juice on the surface very long because the acid in lemon juice can etch the surface.

Walls: Mix a paste of lemon juice and salt. Apply to the spot and wait 15 minutes. Reapply if needed. Prime and repaint if needed.

Wood furniture: Try applying the juice from a fresh lemon as you would for carpet. Do not allow it to set for long because it will warp the wood. Blot. If that begins to dissolve the rust, wait 24–48 hours for the wood to dry, and repeat. The wood might need to be sanded with a 0000 steel-wool pad. Then apply a wood conditioner or refinish if needed.

Salad Dressing

See the section "Grease (Auto) and Motor Oil."

Sap

Automobile: Never use a petroleum distillate on a car as it will damage the finish. Apply baby oil or vegetable oil and give it an hour to loosen the sap. Repeat if needed. Then rinse with sudsy water then again with a vinegar-and-water solution followed by plain water.

Clothing, furniture, and decks: Often the oil from peanut butter will remove tree sap. Dab on a good bit of it, giving it an hour to loosen the sap. Repeat if needed. If that doesn't work, try DeSolvIt, which is found at various department stores.

Hair or hands: Gently rub baby oil or vegetable oil on the sap. Give the oil 5–10 minutes to loosen the sap and wash with warm sudsy water. Repeat if needed.

Scorch Marks

Scorch marks made by irons, cigarette burns, or other forms of heat are not removable. They are burned into the fabric or surface.

If the mark is in wood and is very light, try buffing with a good wax and plenty of elbow grease. Work in the direction of the grain.

Shoe Polish

Carpet: Sponge with a small amount of dry-cleaning solvent, and then blot. Mix 1 teaspoon of a mild detergent containing no alkalis or bleaches with 1 cup of lukewarm water. Blot it on, and then rinse.

Laminated/wood floors and wood furniture: The polish works into the grain of the wood and will be impossible to completely remove. First, try blotting the polish with rubbing alcohol. Wait 15 minutes and blot to remove. Alcohol removes some shoe polishes but not all of them.

If that does not bring the desired results, apply a bit of turpentine. If the polish remains, it has soaked into the grain and the wood must be sanded and refinished.

Fabric furniture and mattresses: Try blotting with rubbing alcohol, and then use DeSolvIt, which is found at hardware stores. Apply, wait 30 minutes, rinse with sudsy water, and then rinse with vinegar and water.

Leather/vinyl: Contact the manufacturer for instructions.

Soot

Fireplace fronts: First, wash the bricks with a strong detergent like Bi-O-Kleen or Seventh Heaven and a good stiff-bristle brush. After cleaning (be sure to put down plastic to protect all surfaces), spray the bricks thoroughly with a can of organic foaming bath cleaner. Saturate the bricks thoroughly and wait 30 minutes; then wash again with sudsy water. Bricks are very porous, and most cleaners saturate through the bricks. A foaming bath cleaner adheres to the surface of the bricks, giving the cleaner time to dissolve the soot.

Walls: A chemically treated dry sponge quickly removes soot from walls without leaving a residue. The sponge is used dry and wiped across the wall. This is the same way professional cleaners wipe down walls after a house fire.

Fabric furniture: First, wipe the furniture with a chemically treated dry sponge. Use the sponge dry and keep moving it so as not to spread the soot to other parts of the item. Then clean the item with a foaming furniture cleaner, testing an inconspicuous spot first.

Stickers

Cars: Grab your hair dryer and heat the sticker until the adhesive softens and the sticker can be removed with a cloth dampened in sudsy water.

Plastic: Apply peanut butter. Allow the peanut butter to remain on the label only long enough to allow the label to be rubbed off. Wipe away excess fluid immediately, wash the article in sudsy water, and dry.

Glass, mirrors, and metals other than aluminum: Fold a paper towel or cloth to make a thick pad as large as the label. Dampen the pad with liquid dish soap and lay it over the label. (Use masking tape to hold the pad onto a vertical surface.) Wait $\frac{1}{2}$ hour to 2 hours, redampening the pad if it dries out. The label will slide off.

Aluminum: Heat with a hair dryer and wipe off. If any residue remains, use a metal polish such as Met-All or Flitz to remove the rest.

Suntan Lotion

See the section "Grease (Auto) and Motor Oil."

Tar

See the section "Glue and Adhesive."

Urine

Carpet and mattresses: When urine hits the padding in carpet, it spreads. What looks like a small stain on the surface is twice that large on the padding. Always treat an area two to three times as large as the surface stain; otherwise the odor will remain and the pet will continue to return to the same spot. Pour on plenty of an enzyme cleaner such as Bac-Out, which is an enzyme product that gets rid of the stain and banishes the odor as well. The enzymes "eat" the odor-causing bacteria.

Fabric furniture: Remove as much of the urine from the furniture as you can with a wet or dry vac. Then soak the seat cushion with Bac-Out. If that doesn't work, you may need to replace the padding in your fabric furniture.

Laminated/wood floor: Dab on a small amount of Bac-Out or Nature's Miracle. Let that set no longer than 5 minutes. Rinse with $1/2$ cup white vinegar per quart of water and dry immediately.

Leather/vinyl: Use a solution of 1 part bleach-free liquid enzyme laundry detergent to 30 parts water. Rinse by blotting with distilled water. Blot to remove excess water, and then dry with air from a fan.

Vomit

See the section "Urine."

Dirty Words

Never use ammonia on plastic or aluminum. Ammonia will interact chemically with either material and can "burn" the aluminum or plastic.

Water Spots

Carpet: Mix a thin paste of baking soda and 3 percent hydrogen peroxide. Gently blot on the spot. Wait 30 minutes and spray with straight peroxide. Allow to dry, brush off what you can, and vacuum to remove the rest. Repeat if needed. Rinse with the vinegar-and-water solution.

Fabric furniture and mattresses: Pour a bit of baking soda on the spot, and then spray with 3 percent hydrogen peroxide. Wait 30 minutes and spray again with peroxide. Wait until the baking soda has dried; then rinse. Repeat if needed. Sometimes water stains on fabric furniture can be removed with straight 3 percent hydrogen peroxide.

Glass shower doors: Open the window, turn on a fan, and ventilate the room. Bring some white vinegar to a boil. Put on a pair of rubber gloves and, with a clean sponge, thoroughly saturate the glass door with the vinegar. Keep repeating this every 15 minutes for an hour. Dampen a white scrub pad (do not use any other color pad because they are more aggressive and will scratch the glass) with the vinegar and add some baking soda to the pad. Scrub the door.

This should remove the whitish look of the water spots. It might need to be repeated depending on the severity of the spots. When water is allowed to stand on a surface, the alkali etches into the surface. The etching is permanent and cannot be removed. A bar of kaolin clay, which is used for removing impurities from cars, might also help to remove the water spots.

Laminated/wood floors: Water damage on hardwood floors generally happens because a pet urinates on the floor or the water has run over after watering a plant. Laminated floors do not stain as easily as wood floors. Absorb as much moisture as possible with a terry towel. Then pour cornstarch on the spot to absorb even more. Press the cornstarch into the floor and replace it with fresh cornstarch as it becomes moistened.

Linoleum: Water damage will look gray or nearly black as it does in wood floors. It cannot be removed from linoleum floors.

Marble and granite: Unless marble and granite are dried immediately after spilling liquid on the floor or damp mopping, water spots will form on the surface. They will look just like water spots on windows and glass shower doors. Try gently buffing the floor with kaolin clay. Make certain the clay you purchase is 100 percent kaolin clay and does not contain any other chemicals. Kaolin clay is solid. If the clay you find is in liquid form, it contains other chemicals that will damage the floor.

Should the water spots refuse to budge, contact Fred Hueston at www.ntc-stone.com. Fred is a leading expert in stone floor care and will have a product that safely removes water spots from marble or granite.

Windows: See the advice for glass shower doors in this section.

Wax

Always place a candle on a candleholder. Candles sweat and leave stains on any hard surface. Never move a burning candle; wait until the wax has solidified. Burn smokeless candles only.

Candlesticks: Place in the freezer for one to two hours. The wax chips right off.

Clothing: Freeze the wax with ice in a zippered plastic bag. Chip off as much wax as possible with a plastic scraper. Place the clothing on top of a paper bag with no printing, and then put an all-white paper towel on top of the wax. Set the iron to medium and iron over the wax. The iron melts the wax into the paper bag. (If you use a paper towel or bag with printing, the heat from the iron sets the ink into the fabric.) To remove the color from colored wax, try soaking the garment in straight 3 percent hydrogen peroxide overnight.

Carpet, mattresses, and fabric furniture: Freeze the wax first with an ice cube placed in a zippered plastic bag and scrape off what you can with a plastic scraper. Grab an all-white paper towel. Set your hair dryer to the hottest setting and heat the wax, wiping it up with the paper towel as it melts. Do not use an iron on carpet. Many carpets are made from Olefin, which is polyester or plastic. It does not take long for the heat from an iron to leave ugly scorch marks in the carpet. A hair dryer may take a bit longer, but it works and is safe to use.

Laminated/wood floor and wood furniture: Place a piece of waxed paper over the wax and set your iron to medium hot. Iron the wax for a few seconds. The wax from the waxed paper melts the wax and lifts it from the surface. If a stain remains, you might be able to remove it with hydrogen peroxide or a remover found at candle shops.

Leather/vinyl: Freezing leather and vinyl is the only safe way to remove wax from these surfaces. Any solvents used on either surface will discolor and damage the fabric. If a dye stain is left after the wax is removed, pour a bit of baking soda on the spot and then spray with hydrogen peroxide. The mixture will bubble and fizzle, and sometimes you get lucky and the stain will come out. Let the mixture set on the dye for 15 minutes and rinse. If it doesn't come out, leave the stain alone. Any solvent, soap, or detergent will further damage the leather or vinyl.

Linoleum: Freeze with an ice cube in a zippered plastic bag and scrape off the hardened wax with a plastic scraper. Use a hair dryer set to medium heat to remove any wax that worked down into those little divots. Beware! Any dye left in the floor is permanent. It has seeped into the inner layers and will not come out.

Tile, marble, and granite floors: For granite and marble floors, follow the instructions for linoleum floors. For tile floors, freeze as you would for linoleum floors. Melted wax will penetrate into the open "spores" of the tile. Heating the wax will only drive it deeper into the tile. Instead, boil some water and then place the pan next to you on a hot pad on the floor. Wearing a pair of rubber gloves, dip a clean, soft cloth in the boiling water and immediately apply to the wax. Sometimes the wax will melt into the cloth. Keep a dry cloth handy for fast blotting.

Walls: You can't remove wax from a wall without damaging the wallboard. The safest method is to beg a friend for assistance. Drape a clean cloth over a dust pan and place that immediately under the wax with no wall space between the pad and the wax. This will catch the wax as it drips. Hold a second cloth in your other hand to blot the wax as it melts. Begin heating the wax gently on the low setting of a hair dryer. As the wax melts, catch what you can with the towel you are holding. The dust pan and cloth will scoop up the rest. If a dye stain remains (and it will), seal the wall with a primer and repaint.

Wine

Carpet: Blot 3 percent hydrogen peroxide on the spot, and then wait 5 minutes. Blot on more peroxide if needed; then rinse.

Missed the stain? Mix a 50/50 solution of hydrogen peroxide to water. Spray it on the spot and let it set 15 minutes. Rinse. Repeat if needed. Wine stains that have gone untreated on the carpet might take several treatments to remove.

Fabric furniture: Dampen a clean, white cloth with hydrogen peroxide. Begin at the outer edge of the stain and blot, working toward the center of the stain. This will help prevent the stain from spreading. Wait 10 minutes, and then rinse. Repeat if needed.

Laminated/wood floor: Wipe immediately to prevent the wine from seeping deep into the wood. After wiping, pour some cornstarch onto the stain and press it into the wood. Sweep up and keep applying the cornstarch until the moisture is gone. It's best to leave any stain alone. Adding more moisture at this point might cause a dark stain and warp the wood. Call a professional.

Leather/vinyl: Dampen a white paper towel with hydrogen peroxide and lay it on the spot, weighing it down with something heavy (such as a pan) for 30 minutes. If the stain has improved but still remains, repeat. Mix a paste of baking soda and hydrogen peroxide, and gently rub to remove any stain left in the crevices. White foaming shaving cream might also help to remove the remaining stain. Finally, treat the leather with a good conditioner.

Linoleum: Wipe immediately. If the wine seeps into the linoleum, the stain is permanent. Sometimes an oven cleaner will remove deep stains in linoleum. Just be aware that it will remove the wax from the floor. You can strip and rewax the floor if needed.

Mattresses: Mix a paste of baking soda and hydrogen peroxide and plaster it on the spot. Wait 30 minutes and spray with straight peroxide. Let it dry and wipe off the baking soda. Repeat if needed.

Marble and granite: Wipe off with warm water and dry immediately. Granite and marble generally don't stain.

Tile: Apply hydrogen peroxide to the stain and rinse with a towel saturated with hot water; then dry immediately. After the red wine has seeped into the tile, there's little you can do to remove the stain. You can remove red wine stains in grout with The StainEraser.

Walls: Dab on a bit of hydrogen peroxide. If the stain remains, you need to apply a primer and repaint the wall.

Wood furniture: Blot immediately until no more moisture has soaked into the towel. Press cornstarch on the stain to absorb as much wine as possible. Remove and repeat until the moisture is gone. Wait until the wood has dried, and then apply peroxide. It may be possible to apply a wood stain or use the meat of a walnut or pecan to restore the color. Sanding and refinishing the surface might be necessary.

B

Your Complete Resource Guide

This appendix is your guide to products mentioned in this book. It also lists places to buy natural products like carpeting and paint, available agencies to help you go natural, and a few other suggestions to peak your green sleuthing skills.

Product Guide

Advantage: Mary Moppins www.goclean.com.

AlumiBrite: www.goclean.com.

Bac-Out: Health food stores.

Benya: See glass cleaners.

Bi-O-Kleen: Health food stores.

Bio Ox: Contact the manufacturer for an outlet near you at www. Bio-Ox.com or 1-866-246-6943.

Bon Ami: Any supermarket.

Brown Sheep Shampoo (to wash wool and sweaters): Call 1-800-826-9136 or go to www.brownsheep.com

Cameo: Supermarket cleaning aisle along with silver polishes.

Citric acid: Available in health food stores or at www.nowfoods.com.

CleanEz: www.goclean.com.

The Clean Team: Jeff Campbell's products meet or exceed all Environmental Protection Agency (EPA) and Food and Drug Administration (FDA) requirements to be classified as safe green cleaners; they can be found at www.thecleanteam.com.

DeSolvIt: Found at Wal-Mart, Kmart, and department stores, or go to www.dtep.com/buy-de-solv-it.htm.

Dishwasher soaps: Bi-O-Kleen, Seventh Generation, or Life Tree can be found in health food stores.

Dry sponge: Found at kitchen and bath stores or go to www.goclean.com/_dry-sponge.htm.

Enzyme products: See Nature's Miracle or Bac-Out.

Erase It for Bathrooms: www.goclean.com/erase-it.htm.

Essential oils: I have purchased from the www.mountainroseherbs.com and www.starwest-botanicals.com several times with 100 percent satisfaction; their oils are pure and properly extracted, but do be careful of the oils you buy because cheap oils are diluted; also available at www.aromaticsinternational.com/oils.php.

Filta Kleen ten 35: Increases your gas mileage and prevents water damage from biofuels; found at www.goclean.com.

Flitz: Available at automotive supply stores, by calling 1-800-333-9325, or by visiting www.flitz-polish.com.

Glass cleaners: Benya at www.goclean.com, The Clean Team's Blue Juice at www.thecleanteam.com, or Bi-O-Kleen.

Guardsman Furniture Polish: Found at fine furniture stores.

Horsehair brush: Found at restaurant supply stores or fine clothing stores.

Hydrogen peroxide, 3 percent: Get these at grocery stores and drug stores.

Hydrogen peroxide, 25 percent food-grade: Available at health food stores, but call first for availability.

Kaolin clay: Available at automotive supply stores.

Kleen-Free: Products to kill fleas, lice, bedbugs, and mites on all surfaces including pets; visit www.kleen-free.com; see also PetQuest.com.

Lambswool duster: Found at kitchen and bath supply stores and department stores or online at www.drugstore.com.

Leather cleaner and conditioner: Stocked in western supply stores, at www.goclean.com, and at www.oakwoodusa.net.

Life Tree Automatic Dishwashing Liquid: Get it at natural food stores or by calling 1-800-824-6396.

Met-All: Available at automotive supply stores or call 1-800-835-5578 or visit www.met-all.com to find a dealer.

Motsenbockers Lift Off #3: Carried in hardware stores.

Nature's Miracle: At pet stores or online at www.petsmart.com.

Plastic scraper: Kitchen supply stores carry these.

Restorz-It: Call 1-800-759-4345 or visit www.restorz-it.com.

Seventh Generation: Sold in health food stores or online at www.seventhgeneration.com.

Squeegee: Found in hardware stores or online at www.goclean.com/accessories.htm#ws.

The StainEraser: To find a dealer, visit www.thestaineraser.com or www.goclean.com.

Towel mops: Visit www.goclean.com, which also carries baby diaper material cloths and lint-free towels.

Other Products to Green Your Home

Bedding: www.ecobusinesslinks.com/links/non_toxic_organic_bedding.htm lists ecofriendly bedding and furniture companies.

Earth- and human-friendly products for the home, yard, and garden: Visit Lehman's Non-Electric Catalog (www.lehmans.com), The Vermont Country Store (www.vermontcountrystore.com), or Real Goods (www.realgoods.com).

Eco Mall: An active community for green living, it has links to a large selection of green living products, an activist center, and information; it can be found at www.ecomall.com.

Environmental Home Center: An online source for green building supplies, www.environmentalhomecenter.com.

Garden and yard supplies: Dirt Works is a Northern Vermont company that has a variety of organic supplies and products for home and garden (www.dirtworks.net). Also see:

Native Plant Society	www.plantsocieties.org
Native Plant Conservation	www.newfs.org
National Gardening Association	www.garden.org/home

Green Home: Featured in *The New York Times*, it has a large selection of natural products for the home; www.greenhome.com.

Home remodeling: www.greenhomeguide.org has a wealth of information on going green when you build or remodel.

Hot water heaters: A complete resource guide to "instant" hot water heaters can be found at www.tanklesswaterheaterguide.com.

Insulation: www.goodshepherdwool.com/benefits.htm and en.wikipedia. org/wiki/Wool_insulation have information on natural wool insulation.

Naturally Yours All-Purpose Cleaner: Find it at www.naturallyyoursstore. com.

Paint: Low VOC paint is available from Sherwin-Williams Harmony and Benjamin Moore Pristine EcoSpec. Other nontoxic paint can be found at Earth Easy (www.eartheasy.com/live_nontoxic_paints.htm). This is a good place for information on nontoxic paints. Other nontoxic paints are Bio Shield Paint (www.bioshieldpaint.com), Livos Paint (www.livos.us), Auro Paint (www.aurousa.com), and Old Fashioned Milk Paint Company (www. milkpaint.com).

Personal care products: www.safecosmetics.org lets you check whether the personal care products you use are safe. Click "How safe are your beauty products?," and then click the tab labeled "Skin Deep."

Sustainable living: A book called *Country Wisdom and Know How from the Editors of Storey Books* teaches you about sustainable living and how to live off the land. Don't miss this book. It is delightful reading with far too much information to list and costs only $20.

Showerheads: Showerheads that remove chlorine and other toxic chemicals can be found at www.cleanairplus.com, www.Ionizers.org, and www.show-erfilter.biz.

Toys: Green information and child safe toys can be found at www. thedailygreen.com/green-homes/eco-friendly/toys.

Organizations and Sources of Information

Agency for Toxic Substances and Disease Registry: Provides health information to prevent harmful exposures and diseases related to toxic substances (www.atsdr.cdc.gov).

American Council for an Energy Efficient Economy: They rate appliance efficiency (www.aceee.org).

Building Green: The GreenSpec Directory lists 2,100 green products (www. buildinggreen.com).

Cancer Prevention Coalition: Learn to protect yourself and your family from cancer (www.preventcancer.com).

The Center for Disease Control and Prevention: Lists 148 chemicals found in human urine and their dangers (www.cdc.gov/exposurereport).

Childproofing Our Communities Campaign: Dedicated to making the environment safe for children (www.childproofing.org).

Children's Environmental Health Network: Protecting children from environmental hazards. Resource guide/links can be found at www.cehn.org.

Children's Health Protection, from the EPA: Visit yosemite.epa.gov/ochp/ochpWeb.nsf/content/homepage.htm.

Citizens for Safe Carpet: This group can help if you have health problems caused by toxic carpeting (call 513-385-1111).

Consumer Health Organization of Canada: Articles on health and green living (www.consumerhealth.org).

Co-Op America and National Green Pages: Visit www.coopamerica.org/pubs/greenpages.

The Dioxin Homepage: Information on the hazards of dioxin (www.ejnet.org/dioxin).

EnviroLink: Extremely large directory of all environmental organizations (www.envirolink.org).

The Environment Directory: Extensive directory of companies and organizations (www.webdirectory.com).

Environmental Protection Agency: Their online website is www.epa.gov.

Essential Oils—Books: Encyclopedia of Essential Oils by Julia Lawless and *The Directory of Essential Oils* by Wanda Sellar.

Friends of Earth: Visit their website at www.foe.org.

The Global Campaign for Recognition of Multiple Chemical Sensitivity: Excellent information can be found at www.mcs-global.org.

Green Seal of Approval: www.greenseal.org/ evaluates products for the Green Seal standard.

Greener Choices: Consumer Reports Guide to green products is found at www.GreenerChoices.org.

Healthy House Institute: An excellent resource for healthy indoor living is available at www.healthyhouseinstitute.com.

Holistic Moms Network: Moms supporting moms who are raising their children in holistic ways (www.holisticmoms.org).

Mother Earth News: An excellent resource magazine for our green environment is online at www.motherearthnews.com.

National Environmental Health Association: Check out their website at www.nfpa.org.

National Institute of Health: Find them at www.nih.gov.

Oregon Department of Environmental Quality: Eliminate toxic substances by downloading an A-Z guide to household hazardous substances at www.Oregon.gov/DEQ. Click "Quick Links" and then click "Hazardous Waste."

Organic.org: An organic online website is at www.organic.org.

Organic Consumers Association: Their website can be found at www.organic-consumers.org.

Organic Trade Association: Visit their website at www.ota.com/index.html.

Physicians for Social Responsibility: Reports on toxic threats to child developmental disorders (www.igc.org).

Recycling: A business resource guide to major recycling programs and companies (www.webdirectory.com/Recycling).

Simple Living: Resources to help you simplify your life (www.ecobusinesslinks.com/simple_living_simple_life.htm).

Simple Living Network: Resources, books, and articles to simplify your life. You'll love this site, at www.simpleliving.net/main/.

U.S. Consumers Product Safety Commission: Check out their website at www.cpsc.gov.

U.S. Department of Energy: Their website can be found at www.doe.gov.

Women's Voices for the Earth: An organization educating women on toxic products (www.womenandenvironment.org).

Index